CONTENTS

Animal Performance

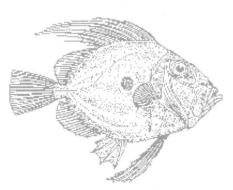

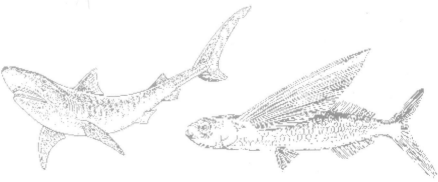

ANIMAL PHYSIOLOGY BOOK 4 EDITED BY DAVID ROBINSON

THE S324 COURSE TEAM

COURSE TEAM CHAIR

David Robinson

COURSE MANAGERS

Alastair Ewing
Colin Walker

AUTHORS FOR BOOK 4

Mandy Dyson
David Robinson

OTHER CONTRIBUTORS

Quentin Bone (Plymouth Marine Laboratories)
Anthony Cassidy
Bob Cordell
Mary Cotterrell (Chester College)
Peter Davies (University of Nottingham)
Marion Hall
Tim Halliday
Robin Harding
Jean Holley
Richard Holmes
David Hoole (University of Keele)
Ian Johnston (University of St Andrews)
Colin Jones (University of Oxford)
Richard Jurd (University of Essex)
Caroline Pond
Monty Priede (University of Aberdeen)
Jeremy Rayner (University of Bristol)
Stewart Richards (Wye College)
Jonathan Rosewell
Jennie Simmons
Ted Taylor (University of Birmingham)
Alison Tedstone (London School of Hygiene and Tropical Medicine)
Jeff Thomas
Nia Whiteley (University of Birmingham)

EDITORS

Perry Morley
Joanna Munnelly
Gillian Riley
Bina Sharma

DESIGN

Martin Brazier
Debbie Crouch

ILLUSTRATION

Janis Gilbert
Mike Gilkes
Pam Owen

INDEX

Jean Macqueen

BBC

Hendrik Ball
Sandra Budin
Andrew Crilly
Mike Gunton
David Jackson
Aileen Llewellyn
Ian Thomas
Nicholas Watson
Barrie Whatley

COURSE SECRETARY

Yvonne Royals

ASSESSORS FOR BOOK 4

Dr Michael Greenwood (University of Derby)
Professor Paul Racey (University of Aberdeen)

The Open University, Walton Hall, Milton Keynes MK7 6AA

First published 1997

Edited, designed and typeset by the Open University

Printed in the United Kingdom by Henry Ling Ltd, at the Dorset Press, Dorchester, Dorset

ISBN 0 7492 5138 7

This text forms part of an Open University Third Level Course. If you would like a copy of *Studying with the Open University*, please write to the Course Reservations and Sales Centre, PO Box 724, The Open University, Walton Hall, Milton Keynes, MK7 6ZS. If you have not already enrolled on the Course and would like to buy this or other Open University material, please write to Open University Educational Enterprises Ltd, 12 Cofferidge Close, Stony Stratford, Milton Keynes, MK11 1BY, United Kingdom.

S324book4i1.1

CHAPTER I ANIMAL PERFORMANCE

1.1 Introduction

This book is about animal performance. Some aspects of animal performance are very impressive. For example, the highest confirmed altitude attained by a bird is 11 277 m. This feat was achieved by a Ruppell's griffon vulture (*Gyps rueppellii*) which collided with a commercial aircraft over the Ivory Coast in 1973. The impact caused one of the plane's engines to be shut down (although the plane subsequently landed safely). The vulture did not survive the collision, though there were sufficient feather remains for a positive identification to be made. The fact that the vulture flew so high was sufficient to obtain it a place in the Guinness Book of Animal Records, but it is not the whole story of the vulture's performance. No mammal of a similar size could breathe enough air to remain conscious at such an altitude. As physiologists, we want to know how the bird takes up oxygen at that altitude, how it conserves the energy that enables it to fly so high, and how it apportions effort into flight and reproduction. We would like to have a picture both of the bird's lifestyle and of its energy budget throughout its existence. Indeed, we might wish to take the analysis further and look at how the bird interacts with both conspecific individuals and with members of other species. Performance is about more than just maximum values for particular variables. Performance encompasses much of whole animal physiology.

The subject of animal performance is too vast to cover in just one book, so in the chapters that follow, we look at just certain aspects of the locomotion of two distinct groups of animals, swimming in fish and flying in vertebrates, in particular, birds. Travel through water and air imposes a number of restrictions on the physiological processes that occur within an animal, and the restrictions in water are different from those in air. However, there are some similarities in the locomotion of animals in these two different media, similarities that are not shared with animals that are exclusively terrestrial. So, in comparing animals living in and moving through water with those living in and moving through the air, the similarities are at least as significant as the differences. Indeed, you will find that some of the theoretical principles of movement are common to both media and, interestingly, there are close methodological links between experiments on flight and experiments on swimming.

Studying animal performance poses a dilemma for the physiologist. Accurate measures of performance can only be obtained from animals that are free in their natural environment, and are in an unstressed state. Yet to measure performance requires the intelligent use of instrumentation and of monitoring techniques; how do you follow a bird through the air or a fish through the oceans? As you read through this book you will encounter a number of ingenious solutions to these challenges. Many of these solutions are the result of modern miniaturization techniques in electronics or the application of sophisticated technology to the unusual requirements of the experimental physiologist. In studying performance, it is as important to know *how* the results were obtained as to know what the results are and how they have been interpreted. In this introductory chapter we consider some of the physical properties of air and water, and show how a concept derived from physics is useful in assessing performance.

1.2   The fluid environment

Although this book is concerned only with those animals such as fish and birds that live predominantly out of contact with solid substrates, you should remember that all animals are in contact with one or other fluid medium. The two fluids are water and air – a liquid and a gas.

■   What is the key characteristic that distinguishes solids from fluids?

A solid has stiffness. The *amount* by which it is deformed if a force is applied is proportional to the magnitude of the applied force. In contrast, when fluids deform, the *rate* of deformation is proportional to the magnitude of the applied force. So, if you apply a constant force to a solid, it deforms to a fixed extent but applying a constant force to a fluid produces deformation at a constant rate.

■   From your own experience, can you give two differences in the physical characteristics of air and water?

Water is a much more *dense* medium than air, and it is more *viscous*. Both these properties influence movement through these fluids and before considering their effects on biological systems, you need to remind yourself of some physics.

1.2.1   Density

The weight of an animal in air is the product of its mass and g, the acceleration due to gravity. The weight of the animal in water is less, due to an upthrust from the water, by an amount equal to the weight of the water displaced by the animal. So, the upthrust is equal to the volume of the animal multiplied by the mass per unit volume of the water, i.e. the **density** of the water.

Air has a density of 1.18 kg m^{-3}. As you would predict, this figure is substantially lower than that of water. Freshwater has a density of $1\,000$ kg m^{-3} and seawater has a density of $1\,026$ kg m^{-3}.

■   Why is seawater more dense than freshwater?

The dissolved salts in seawater give it a greater density. Most marine animals have evolved with a density that is only slightly greater than that of seawater. More accurately, their skeletons are more dense, as are their muscles, but the lipids and any gases in their bodies are less dense. In fact, some marine animals have evolved with a density equal to that of seawater and so neither rise nor sink in it. You will read more about such buoyancy mechanisms in Chapter 4.

1.2.2   Viscosity

The rate at which a fluid is deformed by a force is dependent upon the **viscosity** (resistance to movement) of the fluid. Water is much more viscous than air and, for example, the pressure required to move water through a particular tube is $2\,500$ times that required to move air through the same tube. The viscosity of water at $20°$ C is 55 times greater than that of air. Notice that the temperature is given. Viscosity is related to temperature, and interestingly, water and air show different relationships. As temperature increases, the viscosity of air increases but that of water *decreases*.

As an animal moves through a fluid, the flow of fluid along the body surface exerts a frictional force on the surface, called **drag**. The size of this force is, in part, determined by the way in which the molecules of fluid flow over the surface. If the molecules flow smoothly in layers – *laminar flow* – the frictional force is low. If the molecules flow in a non-linear fashion – *turbulent flow* – the frictional force is greater. As you will appreciate from a knowledge of car, boat and aircraft design, a streamlined body gives a better performance, and this is because it encourages laminar, rather than turbulent flow. However, it is important to note that although it is generally true that turbulent flow is disadvantageous, there are certain circumstances where a degree of turbulence might improve performance. You will read about these later in Section 2.3.1.

An interesting demonstration of the value of reducing turbulent flow is found in dolphins. If the power output of dolphins is calculated, the resulting value appears to be less than that needed to overcome the frictional forces, which clearly cannot be the case. In fact, it has been discovered that the skin has drag-reducing features that prevent turbulence building up and so frictional forces are reduced. The skin appears to damp out any instabilities in the water flowing past that might lead to turbulent flow. This feature is termed **compliance**. Some sharks also seem to have skin with adaptations to drag reduction, for example hammerhead sharks that can swim as fast as 70 km h^{-1}.

The ease with which turbulent flow occurs within a fluid is directly related to the viscosity; the higher the viscosity, the greater the tendency to turbulent flow. There is also a greater tendency for turbulence to develop as velocity increases.

1.3 Animal–fluid interactions

The amount of energy that an animal uses in moving through a fluid is partly dependent on the flow pattern that it creates within the medium, and the flow pattern is a consequence of the relationship between several physical characteristics.

■ Name four physical characteristics, either of the body of the animal or of the fluid, that affect how the animal moves.

You should be aware of:

(a) the density of the fluid (Section 1.2.1);

(b) the viscosity of the fluid (Section 1.2.2);

(c) the shape of the body of the animal (Section 1.2.2).

In addition, you might have realized that the fourth was

(d) the velocity of the fluid relative to the animal.

From these four characteristics can be derived a ratio that describes how fluid flows around a body. This ratio, which has its origins in fluid mechanics, is normally represented by the symbol R_e and is called the **Reynolds number**.

1.3.1   Applying Reynolds number

The Reynolds number is calculated from the following equation:

$$R_e = r \times V \times l/m \tag{1}$$

where r is the density of the fluid, V is the velocity of the body through the fluid, l is determined by the shape of the body and m is the viscosity of the fluid.

R_e represents the ratio between inertial force (determined by the components of the numerator) and viscous force (determined by the denominator). If you imagine a small blob of a substance propelled through water, it will tend to keep moving as a result of inertia but be gradually slowed down by the viscosity of the water. The ratio between these two forces is R_e. Since it is a ratio, it has no dimensions and is described by just a number. R_e is of interest in whole animal studies as it indicates how the performance of an animal moving through a fluid is affected by both the size and shape of its body, and by its surface properties. Measurements of R_e for a range of animal species have shown values ranging from less than 10^{-6} to more than 10^8. Unicellular animals have a low R_e and the viscosity of the fluid is the predominant factor in determining its exact value. In contrast, a large marine mammal moving at high speed has a high R_e and inertia is the predominant factor.

R_e also informs us about how the fluid is affecting the surface of the animal. For example, at low R_e the friction of the skin would be the most important factor in determining its exact value but the density of the fluid would only have a marginal effect.

■   If a particular animal had an R_e of 0.01 in air, into what range would the R_e fall for the same animal in fresh water at 20° C?

The density of fresh water at 20° C is 1 000/1.18 times that of air, i.e. 847 times as dense (Section 1.2.1). Water is 55 times more viscous than air, at this temperature (Section 1.2.2). Using these figures, the R_e in freshwater is roughly $0.01 \times 847/55$ (0.154) as great as that in air, which means that the animal would have an R_e about 15 times greater in water. If the animal had the same R_e in water, then it would swim 15 times slower or be 15 times smaller than in air.

Knowledge of R_e for a particular set of conditions is also required in studies of flight dynamics using a wind tunnel. Similarly, experiments on the hydrodynamics of fish have been carried out by mounting a model fish in a wind tunnel. Provided the R_e is the same in the airstream as it would be in water, the airflow around the model will be dynamically the same as the flow of water around the real fish.

■   Would you expect the model to be larger or smaller than the real fish?

To keep the R_e the same in air as in water, the model would be larger than life. You might also expect the velocity of the air to be greater than the velocity of the water.

1.3.2   A matter of scale

The power produced by a swimming fish is directly proportional to its muscle mass and will usually relate directly to its body mass also. So, for a particular shape of fish, a larger body mass will mean that the frictional force or drag per unit mass will decrease, for the same velocity.

■   What is the reason for drag per unit mass decreasing as mass increases?

Cross-sectional area and surface area, which determine drag, increase with the square of a linear dimension whereas body mass, and hence power, increase by the cube of that dimension. This means that a small difference in body length or width will result in a proportionally greater difference in power than in drag. As a result, a large animal can produce a substantial power output in excess of that needed to overcome drag and so move with a much greater velocity than an animal of identical shape but smaller size.

The higher viscosity and density of water, compared with air, means that the drag forces in water are greater than those in air. Aquatic animals can only match the speed of birds if they are much larger and heavier, and produce a greater power output. However, this is not the whole story, since birds are much more dense than the air in which they fly whereas fish are close to the density of the water in which they swim. So birds must utilize a lot of energy to stay aloft.

If the power output to drag ratio is calculated for a range of aquatic animals, it turns out that the maximum velocities that they can reach are of the order of ten to fifteen body lengths per second, irrespective of their size. So, a unicellular organism swims at about the same rate as a mackerel, in body lengths per second, although the speed of one is measured in mm h^{-1} and the other in km h^{-1}.

1.4   Conclusion

This chapter has dealt with the movement of animals through fluids and has shown how their performance is related to the physical characteristics of both the fluid and the animal, in particular the patterns of flow set up in the fluid as the animal moves. Long, streamlined bodies permit laminar flow and animals such as dolphins produce almost no turbulence as they swim through the water.

The link between the energetic costs of locomotion and the physics of movement through media will be a continuing theme running through this book. You will study structural adaptations that improve both flight and swimming performance, and consider the physiological adaptations that support them. The subject of performance in terrestrial locomotion is not covered here as it is dealt with in a separate book.

Although there are similarities between the factors influencing locomotion in water and air, in this book we shall deal with the two fluids in separate chapters. The reason for this is a biological one – the substantial differences in body plan and form between the principal swimming vertebrate inhabitants of water, the fish, and the principal flying vertebrates, the birds.

Objectives for Chapter 1

After completing Chapter 1 you should be able to:

1.1   Define and use, or recognize definitions of each of the **bold** terms.

1.2   Give one major distinction between solids and liquids.

1.3   List the key physical properties of fluids that have significance for animals moving through them.

1.4   Give a description (in words) of the Reynolds number and give one example of its value to biologists.

1.5   Relate the mass and dimensions of animals to their velocity through a fluid.

CHAPTER 2   PRINCIPLES OF SWIMMING

Prepared for the Course Team by Mandy Dyson

2.1 Introduction

The aquatic environment was the cradle of life on earth. Now, after 10^9 years of evolution, there are more than 22 000 species of fish, which show a diverse variety of adaptations to meet the requirements of their environment. Although good swimmers are found in many other taxonomic groups, fish are masters of the art of propulsive movement through water. Chapters 2–4 of this book explore some of the ways in which fish swim and how they are suited to the habitats in which they occur. Chapter 2 deals primarily with the variety of swimming styles found in fish. It also focuses briefly on the hydrodynamic interactions that occur between fish and the surrounding water, and on the mechanisms involved in converting work done by muscle into a propulsive force in swimming. Chapter 3 looks at the different types of muscle used to power swimming and explores the relationships between muscle arrangement, physiology and function. The ways in which some fish maintain their position in water against a gravitational force is the subject of Chapter 4.

2.2 Modes of swimming

In all fish, the main body muscles are arranged as discrete segments of muscle, called myotomes, situated on either side of an inner spinal column which is incompressible but flexible. These adjacent blocks of muscle are separated by thin but stiff sheets of collagenous tissue called myosepta (which are similar to the collagenous fascia which link muscles to adjacent tissues in many invertebrates and vertebrates), onto which the individual muscle fibres are inserted. Even in primitive fish the myotomes have a complex shape (see Figure 2.1).

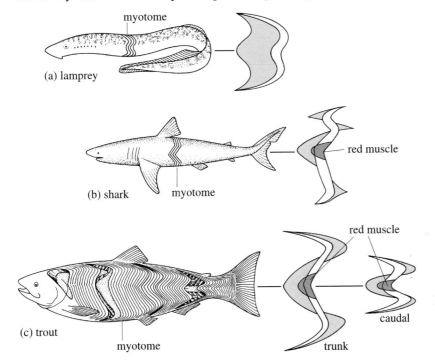

Figure 2.1   The arrangement of the myotomes in three groups of fish. (a) Lamprey (superclass Agnatha), (b) shark (subclass Elasmobranchii) and (c) trout (superorder Teleostei). For the shark (b) and the trout (c) the location of red muscle in the myotome is indicated.

Figure 2.1a and b shows several myotomes in the body of a lamprey and a shark. What we see in this view is the outer surface of the myotome, next to the skin. The three-dimensional structure of a single isolated myotome is shown to the right for each fish, with the surfaces that are normally adjacent to neighbouring myotomes shown in grey. In the trout (Figure 2.1c), several blocks of myotomes have been removed from three different locations to reveal their relationship with the surrounding muscle. To the right are two individual myotomes from the trunk and the tail in the fish body. You can see that, in such teleosts (a superorder which includes most of the bony fishes), the myotomes resemble a series of W-shaped overlapping cones. A single myotome spans many vertebrae between the tips of its anterior and posterior cones. The best way of visualizing the three-dimensional structure of fish muscle is to lightly boil a fish, for example a cod, so that the myotomes can be separated. Most of the muscle is white in colour and is used in burst swimming. The red or brown muscle, located as a small strip near the skin, is used at normal cruising speeds.

As a first step to understanding the role of the myotomes, it is useful to greatly simplify their shape, as shown in Figure 2.2. When the muscle fibres within several adjacent myotomes on one side of the body contract, the body is flexed in that direction. The eel (*Anguilla anguilla*) has a familiar style of swimming (Figure 2.3) but, even in this elementary form of movement, the body is not simply moved from side to side but is thrown into backward-moving waves which pass down the entire length of the body, increasing in amplitude as they do so. Some fish larvae, including herring larvae, swim in a similar way (Figure 2.4). Each locomotion wave is initiated by the contraction of a few anterior myotomes on one side, while the corresponding segments on the opposite side of the column are in a relaxed state and somewhat stretched—the body therefore bends towards the contracted side. The wave so formed then passes backwards, as the myotomal contractions on one side of the fish are propagated in progressively more posterior segments. In Figure 2.4, the crests of such backward-moving waves are indicated by the closed blue circles. Another wave of contraction is initiated anteriorly on the opposite side when the previously relaxed muscles contract and produce a bend in the reverse direction (indicated by the open blue circles) which also moves backwards. Because the bent portions of the body wall push against the water as the wave of contraction moves towards the tail, the fish is propelled forwards. The side-to-side movement of the tail is very pronounced and the 'wasteful' sideways movements at the head mean that this relatively inefficient type of swimming demands a high power output from the body musculature.

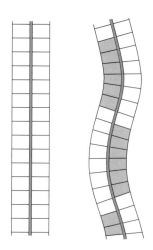

Figure 2.2 A schematic and highly simplified diagram showing how bending of the fish is achieved. Sites of muscular contraction are shown in grey and the spinal column is shown in blue.

Figure 2.3 A mode of swimming typified by the eel (*Anguilla anguilla*). The black silhouette represents a dorsal view of the fish, and the other outlines show the position of the fish 0.3 seconds earlier (in grey) and 0.3 seconds later (in blue).

Figure 2.4 Swimming in the herring larva (*Clupea harengus*) at 0.02-second intervals. The series of black silhouettes shows the movement of a fish relative to a fixed position on the background, which appears as a broken line along the bottom. Movements of the snout and tail tip are indicated by black dots. The crests of the backwardly moving waves of myotomal contraction are indicated by the open and closed blue circles.

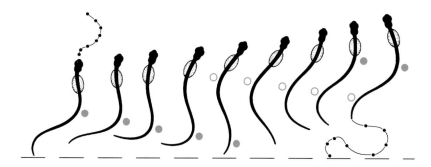

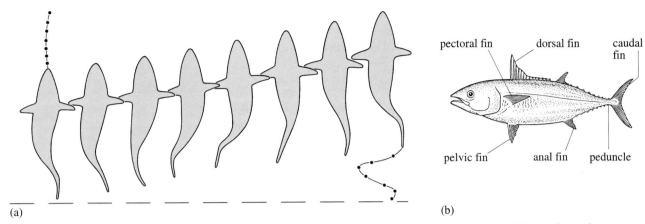

Figure 2.5 (a) Swimming in a skipjack tuna (*Euthynnus affinis*). The diagram is represented as in Figure 2.4, but the intervals are 0.06 seconds. (b) Diagram of a typical tuna showing the major fins. Note the high stiff caudal fin and, immediately in front of it, the slender hind part of the body, called the peduncle, where the hinged joint is located.

Backward-moving waves along the entire body are not evident in fast fish such as mackerel and tuna. These fish appear to generate thrust exclusively by the side-to-side movement of the large tail or caudal fin (see Figure 2.5). Their bodies are less flexible: in tunas, the major body muscles deliver the propulsive force to the tail by large tendons which pull the fan-like tail by moving it back and forth on a hinged joint. The great majority of fish have a mode of swimming intermediate between these two extremes.

■ Why do the myotomes of fish have such complex shapes?

In some fish, one reason is to transfer force efficiently from the mid-body section, where most muscular work is done, to the tail, where thrust is generated against the water. This consideration, however, does not explain why lampreys and eels, which do not have a well defined tail fin, should have complex shapes. Consider Figure 2.6a which shows muscle fibres running parallel to the spinal column (in blue). As the fish bends (Figure 2.6b), the inner fibres nearest the spine do not change length significantly, whereas the fibres near the skin show maximum length change. The parallel arrangement of fibres is therefore impractical since work is shared very unequally between different parts of the myotome. In fact, it has been shown that in order to share work equally, the muscle fibres should run at an angle to the spinal column, but parallel near the skin, with the angle increasing towards the spinal column. Various conical or helical arrangements of muscle fibres are found in different species of fish. They can be compared with the arrangement of fibres in a twisted rope. When a parallel-fibred rope runs round a curve such as a pulley, the outer fibres take most of the strain and are likely to break (Figure 2.6c). Twisted and plaited arrangements of fibres in ropes avoid this problem by ensuring that strain is equalized throughout the rope (Figure 2.6d). In fish, however, muscle fibres do not run throughout the length of the body. Fibres are short, and only run from one myoseptum to the next. The myosepta must be approximately at right angles to the local fibre direction, which means that to accommodate the necessary complex fibre trajectories (Figure 2.7), the myotomes must have a complex shape.

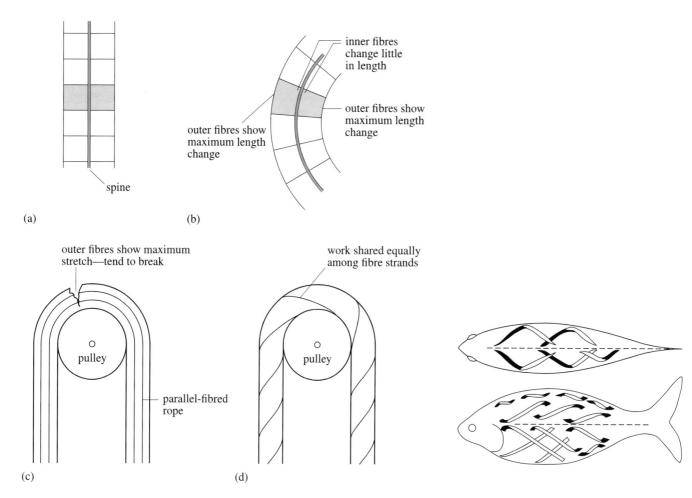

Figure 2.6 (a) and (b) Schematic diagrams of fish myotomes similar to that shown in Figure 2.2. As the fish bends, fibres *parallel* to the spinal column change length by different amounts according to their distance from the spine. (c) A parallel-fibred rope running round a pulley. The outer fibres are stretched the most and tend to break. (d) In a twisted-fibre rope, the fibres are all stretched by a similar amount and the work is shared between the strands.

Figure 2.7 Dorsal and lateral views of a typical teleost fish showing the course of muscle fibres along the body. Note the similarity to the arrangement of fibres in a twisted rope. The myotomes are complex because they must run approximately at right angles to these twisted helical fibre directions.

Summary of Section 2.2

Fish muscle is arranged into discrete segments called myotomes which, even in the most primitive species, are complex in shape. In the eel and some larval fish, backward-moving waves of muscle contraction pass down the length of the body. In fish such as mackerel and tuna, thrust is generated by the side-to-side movement of the large tail fin. The complex shape of the myotomes in these fish facilitates the transfer of force efficiently from the mid-body section to the tail.

2.3 Forces acting on fish

To understand how the work done by the myotomes is converted into a propulsive force in swimming, we first need to consider briefly the forces acting on a body surrounded by water. If the fish is not moving, then gravity (weight) acts in the downward direction and is opposed by **buoyancy** in the upward direction. In most fish the average density of the body tissue is close to that of water. Buoyancy is then roughly equal to the weight, a situation known as **neutral buoyancy**, and there is no tendency for the fish to rise or sink. Buoyancy is also known as **static lift** (Figure 2.8a).

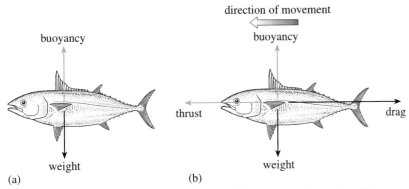

Figure 2.8 (a) In a neutrally buoyant stationary fish, e.g. a tuna, the upthrust from buoyancy exactly equals the weight of the fish. (b) A moving fish must generate forward thrust in order to overcome drag.

2.3.1 Overcoming drag

If the fish is moving, it experiences a force opposing the motion, known as **drag**. In order to move forward, the thrust must exceed the drag. Drag depends on the density and viscosity of the fluid medium. Compared with air, water is both dense and highly viscous and so, for swimming animals, overcoming drag is a serious problem. Drag increases with speed (v) in accordance with the square law.

■ What are the consequences for drag of an increase in speed?

If speed doubles, the drag, and hence the thrust necessary, quadruples. Swimming fast therefore requires the ability to produce vast amounts of thrust in order to overcome drag.

The effects of the drag square law can be seen in Table 2.1. If we express speed in some arbitrary units, e.g. body lengths per second (BL s⁻¹), we can see that in order to travel at 10 BL s⁻¹ requires 100 times the thrust (drag) and 1 000 times the power needed for 1 BL s⁻¹. Power is the rate of energy utilization (joules per second = watts) and the power required gives a good indication of the amount of muscle needed to achieve a given speed. Swimming at 10 BL s⁻¹ requires 1 000 times the muscle mass that swimming at 1 BL s⁻¹ requires. Very large amounts of muscle are therefore needed to swim at very high speeds and the maximum speed of fish is limited by the total mass of muscle available in the body. As much as 60% of body mass can be muscle in some species.

Table 2.1 The drag, power and energy cost of swimming at different speeds.

Speed, v	Drag = thrust, v^2	Power (drag × speed), v^3	Basal power, B	Total power, $v^3 + B$	Energy cost of transport, $(v^3 + B)/v$
0.10	0.01	0.00	1	1.00	10.01
0.50	0.25	0.13	1	1.13	2.25
1	1	1	1	2.00	2.00
2	4	8	1	9.00	4.50
3	9	27	1	28.00	9.33
4	16	64	1	65.00	16.25
5	25	125	1	126.00	25.20
6	36	216	1	217.00	36.17
7	49	343	1	344.00	49.14
8	64	512	1	513.00	64.13
9	81	729	1	730.00	81.11
10	100	1 000	1	1 001.00	100.10

This analysis seems to show that swimming in fish might be very difficult, but it should be noted that to swim at slow speeds requires very little power and hence very little muscle (remember the small quantity of red muscle present in most fish, as shown in Figure 2.1). Since the body weight is supported by buoyancy, underwater swimming at modest speeds by fish is the most economical form of transport known in the animal kingdom. The cost of transport is normally expressed in energy required per unit distance. In Table 2.1 we must first add basal or maintenance metabolism (B) to the power required for swimming to give total power. This sum divided by the speed then gives the cost of transport in the final column (arbitrary units are retained for simplicity).

■ What does this final column show?

It shows that swimming very slowly is moderately costly and swimming very fast is very costly, but there is an optimum range of speeds at which cost is at a minimum.

■ What is the optimum speed for most fish according to Table 2.1?

For most fish the optimum speed is approximately 1 BL s^{-1} and it is this speed that fish should adopt to achieve maximum distance with minimum energy expenditure. It should be noted that swimming at the surface (as humans do) wastes a lot of energy in wave-making and costs about five times as much as underwater swimming. The low energy cost of swimming only applies to submerged swimmers.

Overcoming drag dominates the swimming of fish and so any means of minimizing drag is beneficial and likely to be favoured by natural selection. Drag can be divided into two kinds of effect, **pressure drag** and **skin friction drag**. Pressure drag is the direct force experienced by the fish as it tries to push its way forward through the water. If you ride a motor cycle, you feel this as the pressure of the air on your face and body if you try and sit upright. It is best avoided by crouching down on the motor cycle and minimizing your frontal area. If we imagine a hypothetical primitive spherical fish, it is obvious that drag could be reduced by changing the shape to that of a narrow cigar with minimum frontal area. This suggests that all fish should be long, thin and eel-like. However, increasing the length increases the skin area and therefore the friction drag caused by the water flowing over the body. There are also problems of flow over very elongated bodies. Shapes designed to minimize drag are known as streamlined. Minimum drag is experienced when the width (*w*) to length (*l*) ratio, i.e. the profile thickness, is 0.25 (Figure 2.9a).

This shape is found in most fast-swimming animals and many fish (Figure 2.9b). Drag is further minimized by reducing any protuberances on the body. In tunas, for example, all the fins (except the tail fin) can be folded into grooves or recesses on the body and even the eye is flush with the surface of the head and covered with a transparent layer of fatty adipose tissue.

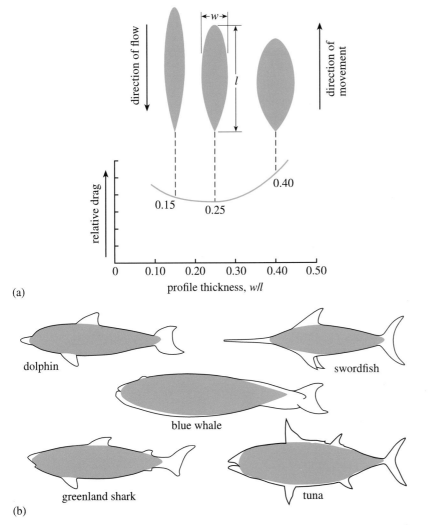

Figure 2.9 The effect of body shape on drag. (a) A width-to-length ratio of 0.25 with a circular cross-section gives minimal drag. (b) Some of the many fish and marine mammals that correspond closely to this shape.

In streamlined fish swimming at low speeds, the flow of water around the body is ordered into layers. A thin layer of water, known as the boundary layer, adheres to the skin and successive layers away from the body are influenced less and less by the movement of the fish. This condition is known as laminar flow and results in relatively low drag. As swimming speed increases, the flow around the body tends to break down and the boundary layer becomes turbulent. The onset of turbulence causes an approximately three-fold increase in drag, which could impose a maximum speed barrier on some species. However, there are several ways in which fish can delay the transition to a turbulent layer. The onset of turbulence usually begins in the tail region and it is thought that, in tunas, the little finlets on the peduncle (Figure 2.5b) help delay the onset of turbulence as speed increases. In fast-swimming fish, lateral movements of the body are reduced—only slow swimmers have body movements of large amplitude. Mucus exuded from fish skin can also reduce the friction and promote laminar flow. Tests on mucus of the Pacific barracuda (*Sphyraena* sp.) suggest that frictional drag might be reduced by almost 66%, but there is no means of verifying this estimate in a living fish. Calculations indicate that reduction of friction by mucus is likely to be most effective at slow speeds. The effect of turbulence, however, can be reduced by deliberately roughening the skin to generate microturbulence. The microturbulent layer next to the skin acts as a sort of lubricating layer reducing frictional drag and delaying the onset of fully developed turbulence. The scales of some fish such as sharks are equipped with little teeth or protuberances 0.05–0.20 mm high that may help promote microturbulence. In some racing yachts it has been found that deliberately roughening the hull may reduce drag.

Some marine fish have a 'porous' skin, with a 'canal' system filled with seawater just under the outer surface, which may help sustain laminar flow. Among the most interesting is the castor-oil fish, *Ruvettus pretiosus*, examined by the British physiologist Quentin Bone. Here, pointed ctenoid scales project above the skin surface and act as 'vortex generators', producing tiny vortices from the tips of the scales which stabilize the boundary layer (Figure 2.10). In addition, this complex skin has sub-dermal spaces that may aid stabilization by sucking in and squirting out seawater as the body moves.

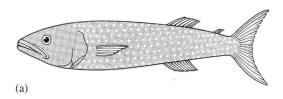

(a)

Figure 2.10   The castor-oil fish (*Ruvettus pretiosus*) and the structure of the skin. (a) The ctenoid scales (shown as white dots). (b) Three-dimensional representation of the pores which are irregularly scattered between the ctenoid scales, and their connection to the relatively large water-filled sub-dermal spaces. (c) A vertical section which suggests how the ctenoid scales might operate as vortex generators. Blue arrows indicate water movement.

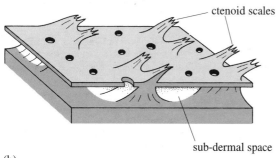

(b)

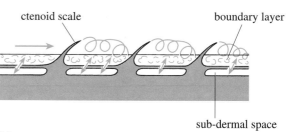

(c)

2.3.2 Generation of thrust

The basic undulating-body swimming motion of fish can be understood by comparing it with a snake crawling through grass. However, this analogy is an oversimplification since water does not remain static as the fish moves forward. In reality, water must be accelerated backwards to generate a force (thrust) propelling the fish forward. Thus, as a fish swims through the water, it leaves a jet of backward-moving water behind it.

If we compare the fish to a toy submarine, it can be seen that the total momentum imparted to the jet of water from the propeller is equal to the thrust force (Figure 2.11a). In fact, wakes of propellers are more complex and fish certainly do not generate a steady jet flow from their tails. Rather,- a series of spinning vortices is shed from the tail (Figure 2.11b, c). Each vortex can be regarded as a packet of water propelled backwards by the sweep of the tail. The direction of the vortex is anti-clockwise during the tail beat to the right and clockwise during the tail beat to the left. The amount of thrust developed depends on the number of vortices shed per second and their magnitude. A single to-and-fro sweep of the tail sheds two main vortices known as a stride. The stride length of most normal fish corresponds to about 0.7 body lengths, i.e. the fish moves forward a distance of 0.7 body lengths for each to-and-fro beat of

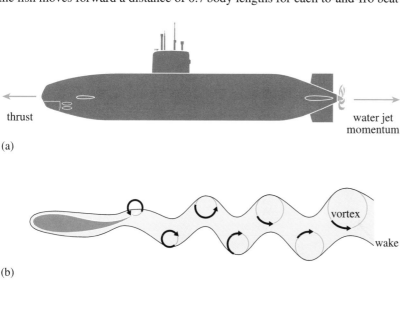

(a)

(b)

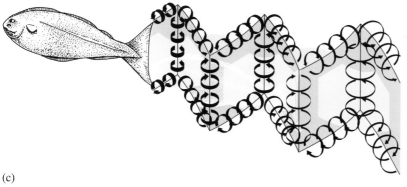

(c)

Figure 2.11 (a) The thrust in a toy submarine is equal to the momentum imparted by the propeller to the water. (b) A two-dimensional view of the wake behind a swimming fish viewed from above. The bound vortices, released at the end of every stroke to the left or to the right, are shown. The arrows indicate the direction of rotation, and their length the relative velocity of the vortices. (c) An impression of the three-dimensional vortex flow system behind a saithe (*Pollachius virens*). The tail blade is shown in the middle of a stroke to the left, i.e. towards you. The thickness of the arrows indicates relative velocity. The velocity decreases and the diameter of the vortices increases with increasing distance from the tail.

the tail. There is, therefore, a simple linear relationship between the tail-beat frequency and the speed of a fish. A further limitation to the maximum speed of fish is the minimum contraction time of the muscles.

The amount of water propelled into the vortex wake is clearly dependent on the size of the tail. The **aspect ratio (AR)** of a fin is defined as *the square of the span of the fin* (i.e. the square of the distance between the tips of the lobes, s^2) *divided by the surface area of the fin* (Figure 2.12). A tail with a high aspect ratio (AR), projecting to a maximum distance above and below the mid-line of the body, will produce the maximum thrust. High-aspect-ratio tails (Figure 2.12a) are found in fish such as mackerels and tunas that swim at a constant high speed. The tails of tunas have an AR of about 6, which is about as high as can be achieved without sacrificing strength. If you imagine such a tail as in Figure 2.12a beating very slowly, the water simply flows around it without having any effect and no thrust is generated because the lower viscosity limit of the tail fin has been reached. In other words, the tail has no 'grip' on the water and it 'stalls'. One solution to this is a broader, low-aspect-ratio tail such as is found in salmon and cod (Figure 2.12b). Such tails are better at slow speeds and for acceleration from a standing start. The tail fin is supported by flexible rays which enable the aspect ratio of the tail to be adjusted as the speed changes. However, at very low speeds the tail fin becomes completely ineffective and the 0.7 body lengths per stride relationship breaks down. The lower viscosity limit of a low-aspect-ratio tail is reached when oscillating at one beat per minute.

The solution for generating thrust efficiently at low speeds is to use rapid undulations of smaller fins accelerating a smaller mass of water. Thus many fish swim by undulating either the pectoral, ventral or dorsal fins or a combination of these.

The rays swim by means of greatly enlarged pectoral fins. Figure 2.13a is a lateral view of a manta ray swimming from left to right. Waves of undulations (in a vertical plane) pass backwards along the fin margins, and a superficial similarity with the mode of flight in birds is striking. Other fish move by the undulations of the dorsal fins. For example, the bowfin (Figure 2.13b) uses only its dorsal fin for gentle forward locomotion, though it can undulate its body for rapid movement during feeding or escape. The knifefish (Figure 2.13c) swims by undulation of an extremely long anal fin. The sea-horse (Figure 2.13d) uses both its dorsal and pectoral fins to generate thrust. The swimming function of the tail has been lost and it has become a grasping organ enabling the fish to hold onto seaweed. The thrust produced by undulating fins can often be reversed or changed in direction, something that is difficult to achieve using the caudal fin. Many fish 'row' themselves or they oscillate small dorsal or pectoral fins. Often such fins are rounded and paddle-like, and beat very rapidly and synchronously, for example, those of the stickleback (Figure 2.13e). The John Dory (Figure 2.13f) moves forward by wave-like movements of the dorsal and anal fins, with the pectoral fins mainly used to provide stability during any manoeuvre. Many of the tropical coral reef fish move exclusively by fins and steer with the caudal fin. The ocean sunfish is a remarkable species, because much of the body musculature has been lost. The tail is a rudder-like hinged flap, and forward locomotion depends on the side-to-side movement of the extraordinarily high dorsal and anal fins (Figure 2.13g). The aspect ratio of the fins is very high and movement in this fish has properly been described as 'a bird flight mode turned through 90°, with high-aspect-ratio wings displayed in a vertical plane'.

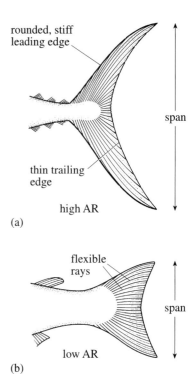

Figure 2.12   Aspect ratios in the caudal fins of two teleosts: (a) a tuna and (b) a cod. AR = span^2/surface area.

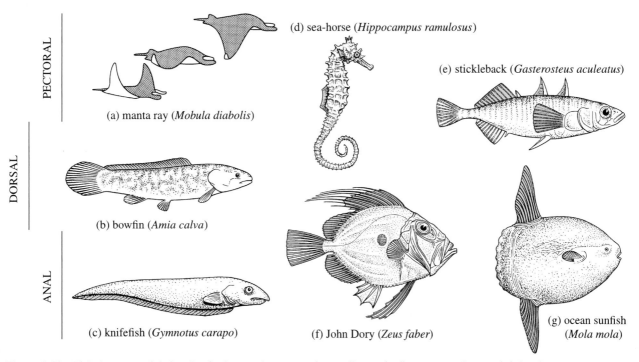

Figure 2.13 Fish that use undulating fins for locomotion grouped according to the fins concerned — see left-hand side of the figure. The relevant fins are shown in blue.

2.3.3 Hydrodynamic lift

Many fish are heavier than water and the static balance diagram shown in Figure 2.8a does not apply. Such fish must create **hydrodynamic lift** to compensate for the net negative buoyancy. Lift can be generated by extending the pectoral fins like wings on either side of the body (Figure 2.14a, b). Viewed from the side, the pectoral fins of a swimming dogfish are slightly inclined to the horizontal, with their leading edge higher than their trailing edge. Under these conditions the fins act as a hydrofoil. If a hydrofoil is to generate lift, it must be inclined, i.e. it must operate at an angle of incidence, α, otherwise the pressure above and below the foil will be equal. With an inclined fin, water moves faster over the upper surface, and this produces a difference in the pressures above and below the foil that lifts the fish upwards. This mechanism is shown schematically in Figure 2.15, where the pressure at the various sites shown in blue on the upper and lower surface of a hydrofoil is indicated by the height of the blue fluid in the manometer tubes. The lift force on a wing or hydrofoil increases with the velocity squared, so that at very low speeds the resulting upward force is small and may not be sufficient to counterbalance weight. Because of this, there is a minimum speed below which a shark or tuna cannot swim without sinking. Mackerel avoid sinking at low speeds by tilting their body upwards. The tilted body provides some extra lift, and swimming forces from the tail are no longer directed horizontally but slightly upwards along the direction of the vertebral column. The tilt angle can be varied in order to increase or decrease speed (Figure 2.16). In sharks and dogfish, lift is also generated by the asymmetric tail, which has a relatively longer, stiff, upper lobe (Figure 2.14a). The tail twists as it moves from side to side, and so generates an upward force as well as forward thrust. Sharks and dogfish therefore do not have to tilt their bodies to create lift.

Chapter 5 looks at how birds' wings act as aerofoils and generate lift for flight.

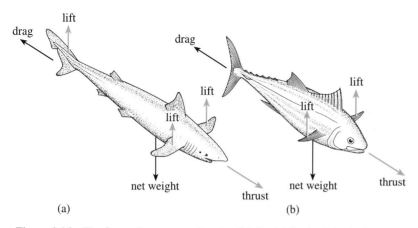

Figure 2.14   The forces that act on swimming fish for (a) the dogfish (*Scyliorhinus* sp.) and (b) tuna (*Thunnus* sp.), both of which are denser than the seawater in which they swim.

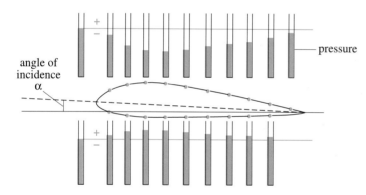

Figure 2.15   The distribution of pressure around a hydrofoil at a positive angle of incidence (α) in a water tunnel. The height of the blue fluid indicates the pressure at the corresponding position on the upper or lower surface of the hydrofoil. Ambient pressure is indicated by the blue lines.

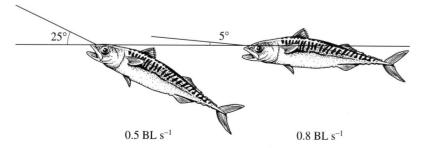

Figure 2.16   The relationship between tilt angle and speed in the mackerel (*Scomber scombrus*).

To create lift efficiently it is better to have pectoral fins with a high aspect ratio. Figure 2.17 shows examples of both elasmobranchs and teleosts that are heavier than water and have high-aspect-ratio pectoral fins.

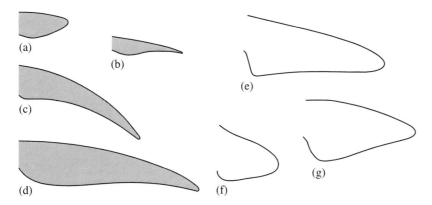

Figure 2.17   The shape of the pectoral fins of a variety of fish, viewed dorsally. The shaded fins to the left are of teleosts: (a) mackerel (*Scomber scombrus*); (b) swordfish (*Xiphias* sp.); (c) carangid (*Trachurus* sp.); (d) longfin tuna (*Thunnus alalunga*). The fins on the right are of elasmobranchs: (e) blacktip shark (*Carcharhinus limatus*); (f) dogfish (*Scyliorhinus* sp.); (g) basking shark (*Cetorhinus* sp.).

In most fish that are adapted to fast and prolonged cruising, the ARs of both the caudal and pectoral fins are high and many such fins are elliptical. However, such fins are not appropriate for rapid acceleration or swift manoeuvring when the angle of incidence must be high—tall thin hydrofoils with a high AR are particularly prone to stalling when the angle of incidence is large. The result is that fish that rely upon rapid acceleration or high manoeuvrability, e.g. salmon, pike, barracuda and cod, have shorter pectoral and large 'spoon-like' caudal fins with lower ARs, which are less susceptible to stalling. You will see in Chapter 5 that the same design principles are relevant to flight: large birds requiring rapid acceleration at take-off (for example, the pheasant) tend to have stubbier wings than birds that are adapted for prolonged cruising (for example, the albatross).

So far we have only considered lift as force acting vertically upwards. Strictly, lift is any force acting at right angles to the direction of motion. Figure 2.11c shows vortices being shed by the tail in generating thrust. The tail can be thought of as an undulating wing generating lift in the sideways direction, first one way and then the other. Since the body of the fish is shaped so as to not move sideways, by appropriate adjustments of the angle of incidence of the fin, a forward component of lift is expressed as thrust.

Summary of Section 2.3

There are several forces that act on a fish surrounded by water. When a fish is stationary, gravity in a downward direction is opposed by buoyancy in an upward direction. In most fish, the average density of the body tissues is close to that of water and the fish is said to be neutrally buoyant. The forward movement of a fish is opposed by drag and so in order to move forward, fish must generate thrust that exceeds drag. There are several means by which fish overcome drag. One of these is by streamlining, another is by reducing protuberances on the body. Thrust is generated by a series of vortices shed from the tail, and the amount of thrust generated depends on the number of vortices shed per second and on their size. This in turn depends on the size of the tail. Tails with high aspect ratios produce maximum thrust and are found in fish that swim at constant high speeds. Low-aspect-ratio tails are better at slow speeds and for acceleration from a standing start. Some fish are heavier than water and so must generate hydrodynamic lift in order to compensate for net negative buoyancy, and there are several ways in which this is achieved.

2.4 Energy expenditure during swimming

Although it is possible to measure the swimming speeds of fish in the wild using telemetry, energy expenditure estimates are generally derived from basic measurements made on fish that are exercised at known speeds in the controlled environment of a swimming chamber—the aquatic equivalent of a treadmill. There is a wide variety of ingenious swimming chamber designs, but an arrangement in which the fish swims against a water current within a stationary chamber known as a water tunnel, is most widely used (Figure 2.18). The water current is generated by gravity flow or a pump. The practical problems of their design are considerable: minor currents and excessive turbulence have to be avoided, friction can warm up the water of the chamber and the fish have to be confined to a limited section. (A light source can act as a visual cue and mild electric shocks can restrict the fish). If the total volume of water in a swimming chamber is fairly small, changes in the concentration of dissolved gases can be accurately monitored by an oxygen electrode and the rate of oxygen consumption by the fish gives us measurements of metabolic rate and energy expenditure at various swimming speeds.

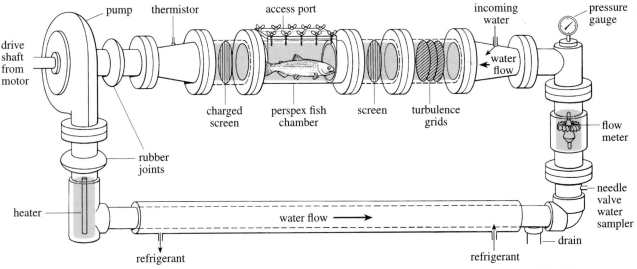

Figure 2.18   A tunnel respirometer used to measure oxygen consumption in sockeye salmon (*Oncorhynchus nerka*). The fish swims 'upstream' against a water flow that can be varied. If the fish moves slower than the flow of water, it slips back onto an electrically charged screen. Water temperature can be varied and, when the system is closed and a fixed volume of water circulated, the reduction in oxygen content of the water can be calculated.

Figure 2.19 shows the relationship between oxygen consumption and swimming speed in Pacific sockeye salmon. The data were obtained over 30 years ago by John Brett using this apparatus. The fish used had been kept at the experimental temperature for a long time beforehand and so were acclimated or adapted to it. Oxygen consumption is shown as the continuous blue line and the 'at rest' metabolic rate by the dashed black line. It is clear that metabolism increases approximately exponentially with increased swimming speed (Figure 2.19a). This is because the power required for swimming increases with velocity in an approximately cube law relationship (Table 2.1). Maximum oxygen consumption is about $630\,cm^3\,O_2\,kg^{-1}\,h^{-1}$ when the salmon swims at about $4\,BL\,s^{-1}$. This high level of energy expenditure can be sustained for long periods and is the greatest metabolic rate that can be fully supported by aerobic metabolism. So, $630\,cm^3\,O_2\,kg^{-1}\,h^{-1}$ represents the **aerobic capacity** of the fish which, as we shall soon see, is of great interest to physiologists concerned with animal performance.

So far we have talked only of sustained swimming in the salmon, supported by aerobic metabolism. However, during brief bursts, speeds well in excess of $4\,BL\,s^{-1}$ are attainable and the extra energy is supplied anaerobically. After such bursts, additional oxygen, known as **recovery oxygen**, is taken up to complete the oxidation of substrates only partially oxidized by anaerobic metabolism. The amount of recovery oxygen taken up for the salmon can be estimated from Figure 2.19a. By extending the continuous blue line (the dashed section), we can estimate the theoretical demand for oxygen at swimming speeds greater than $4\,BL\,s^{-1}$. However, the amount of oxygen actually consumed at these speeds is at the maximum level (about $630\,cm^3\,kg^{-1}\,h^{-1}$). The blue area shown in Figure 2.19a represents the difference between the total energy needed and the smaller amount supplied by aerobic means at speeds above $4\,BL\,s^{-1}$. As Figure 2.19a implies, the amount of recovery oxygen required is very modest at speeds less than $4\,BL\,s^{-1}$ and not sufficient to interfere seriously with the fish's performance.

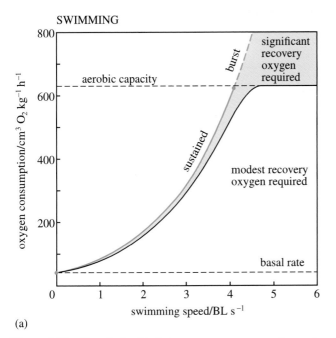
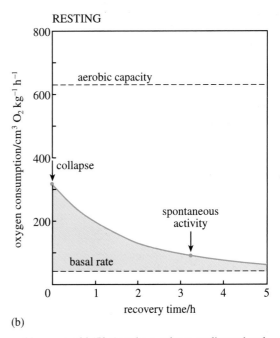

Figure 2.19 The relationship between oxygen consumption and swimming speed in a year-old (50 g) sockeye salmon acclimated and tested at 15 °C. The continuous blue line shows oxygen consumption during (a) increasing swimming speeds, and (b) a resting phase of recovery after burst swimming in excess of $4\,BL\,s^{-1}$. Above $4\,BL\,s^{-1}$ significant recovery oxygen is required.

At high speeds, the utilization of the limited stores of glycogen restricts the length of burst swimming, and the duration of bursts decreases as their speed increases. Speeds of about 5–6 BL s^{-1} can be maintained for only a few minutes. The time taken for the uptake of recovery oxygen can be estimated by measuring oxygen consumption after the completion of burst swimming; when O_2 consumption returns to pre-exercise levels, and when muscle glycogen and lactate are restored, sufficient oxygen has been taken up. During recovery in the sockeye salmon, the fish rests quietly on the bottom with little visible movement, other than pronounced hyperventilation, for as long as 2–3 hours (see Figure 2.19b). Uptake of sufficient recovery oxygen may take more than 5 hours, although spontaneous movement may begin again after 3 hours. Recovery from intense burst swimming in mackerel may take up to 24 hours. We are unsure why recovery from burst swimming is so slow. In the wild, prolonged inactivity would be a serious handicap because exhausted fish are vulnerable to predation. This probably explains why fish are extremely reluctant to move at high speed unless the motivation is strong and, under natural conditions, intense burst swimming is probably a rare event.

The most significant environmental factor influencing the metabolic activity of fish is temperature, though the precise effect differs from species to species. To show this, the data in Figure 2.19a can be replotted on semi-logarithmic co-ordinates, so they now appear as a straight line. In Figure 2.20 the blue line labelled 'sockeye 15 °C' simply replots the values shown in Figure 2.19a and the other lines give data at different temperatures (5 °C and 20 °C for the salmon) and for a number of different species.

■   What does the graph show?

Within a single species, for example the sockeye salmon, the differences in the slope of the lines at various temperatures show that the extent to which oxygen demand is raised as swimming speed increases, varies with ambient temperature. It also shows that when both basal and maximum rates of metabolism are measured at the same temperature, there are considerable differences between species. For example, compare bass and salmon at 20 °C: the bass has a maximum oxygen consumption less than half that of the salmon, and at this point could reach speeds of only 2.4 BL s^{-1} as compared with 3.6 BL s^{-1} for the sockeye salmon.

Two further points emerge from Figure 2.20:

1   Because the salmon is a poikilotherm its metabolism increases as the animal is warmed, resulting in greater oxygen demand (compare basal metabolism at 5, 15 and 20 °C). However, at elevated temperatures, water holds less dissolved oxygen so warm fish must ventilate a much greater volume of water over their gills. When salmon migrate from the oceans to what may be warmer rivers for migration upstream, their energy expenditure must increase substantially.

2   *Tilapia* is a poikilothermic warm-water species. If fish showed a simple relationship between metabolic rate and temperature, then the basal metabolic rate of *Tilapia* at 25 °C would be considerably greater than that of the salmon at 20 °C, which is not the case. Indeed, the oxygen demand of a *Tilapia* swimming at 1 BL s^{-1} at 25 °C is about the same as that of the sockeye salmon swimming at the same speed at 15 °C. We are very uncertain of the biochemical basis of such differences in poikilotherms.

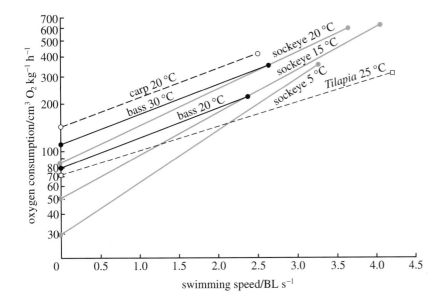

Figure 2.20 The relationship between oxygen consumption and swimming speed for a variety of fish at different temperatures. For each species, O_2 consumption (on a logarithmic scale) is shown up to the maximum sustainable speed. Data from the sockeye salmon are shown in blue for three different water temperatures and those for the bass (*Micropterus salmoides*) at two temperatures (20 °C and 30 °C). Oxygen consumption of the carp (*Cyprinus carpio*) and *Tilapia nilotica* was measured at different swimming speeds at 20 °C and 25 °C, respectively.

2.4.1 Aerobic metabolic scope

So far, we have used the data on salmon in Figure 2.19 to identify a basal rate of metabolism (about $42 \, \text{cm}^3 \, O_2 \, \text{kg}^{-1} \, \text{h}^{-1}$) and a maximum rate of O_2 consumption—the aerobic capacity ($630 \, \text{cm}^3 \, O_2 \, \text{kg}^{-1} \, \text{h}^{-1}$). The difference between these two values reflects the maximum amount of energy that is available to support work or activity over and above that necessary for normal 'routine' energy requirements (for example, growth and reproduction) and is termed the **aerobic metabolic scope**. It gives an indication of the capacity of an animal to support activity by aerobic methods. If we are concerned with the total energy that an animal can make available for work or activity, we have to add a second component, anaerobic metabolic scope, which is limited by the size of the muscle store of glycogen and by the maximum rate of lactic acid formation by glycolysis.

Aerobic metabolic scope is a useful idea but it is not as simple as it seems, and one major limitation is evident from work with fish. Measuring capacity for work in the way just described assumes that the energy-requiring processes that occur when the fish is resting do not increase in magnitude once the fish becomes active. This assumption is clearly untrue—the ventilatory and circulatory systems increase their work output and, at maximum swimming speeds, they may account for as much as 40% of the increased oxygen uptake.

The necessity of accounting for such 'maintenance' costs is one of many reasons why we should view aerobic metabolic scope only as an indicator of the extent to which animals can increase aerobic metabolism and not as an indirect measure of an animal's capacity to perform work. However, when we look at a single species, or at a group of closely related species, the maximum oxygen consumption can be closely linked with maximum performance and here differences between species in aerobic metabolic scope do parallel differences in the capacity of different fish to perform work.

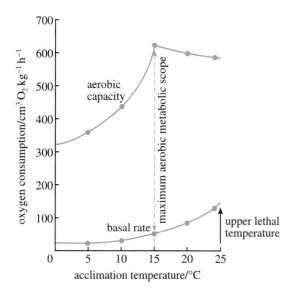

Figure 2.21   The relationship between oxygen consumption and acclimation temperature in a year-old sockeye salmon. The lower line shows the 'basal' rate of oxygen consumption at different acclimation temperatures. The upper line shows the maximal oxygen consumption that can be elicited by activity (i.e. the aerobic capacity) at different acclimation temperatures.

The type of diagram shown in Figure 2.21 is useful if we want to compare oxygen consumption at different states of activity and at different temperatures. Basal metabolism and aerobic capacity have been measured in the sockeye salmon at a variety of water temperatures. The upper line shows the maximum O_2 consumption at peak sustainable speeds after acclimation at different ambient temperatures. The scope for aerobic metabolism is indicated by the vertical distance between the two lines. Figure 2.21 shows clearly that in the salmon the scope is greatest at 15 °C. The highest temperature that the salmon can tolerate is the upper lethal temperature—25 °C. The general features shown in Figure 2.21 for the sockeye salmon are evident in many other fish species. In particular, the maximum aerobic metabolic scope is exhibited at some optimum temperature (15 °C for the sockeye salmon) above and below which the scope is smaller. Many poikilothermic animals have a 'preferred' body temperature, which is normally maintained by behavioural means in the wild and which may conform to the temperature at which aerobic metabolic scope is maximal.

It is very instructive to compare the aerobic capacities and scopes of different groups of animals, though any generalizations must be framed cautiously. Ideally we should compare species of approximately similar size because differences in body mass alone have a major effect on metabolism. In general though, more active fish have higher aerobic metabolic scopes and higher aerobic capacities than less active fish. It is even more interesting to compare teleosts with reptiles. For example, Figure 2.22 shows the maximum and minimum O_2 consumption at various temperatures for three species of lizard, together with the now-familiar data for the sockeye salmon (shown in blue). The most striking feature here is that despite the lizards' air-breathing habit, their aerobic capacities and scopes are not greatly different from those of the fish. In fact, the salmon has a higher capacity and scope than either the bearded dragon or the iguana. Some reptiles normally maintain by day a body temperature quite close to that of homeotherms, and such animals tend to live at a higher metabolic rate than most fish. Nonetheless, most lizards display short bursts of activity supported mostly by anaerobic glycolysis, separated by longer bouts of rest and relative quiet, when metabolism is largely aerobic. Of the lizards shown in Figure 22.2, the monitor lizard is large and predatory and has an aerobic

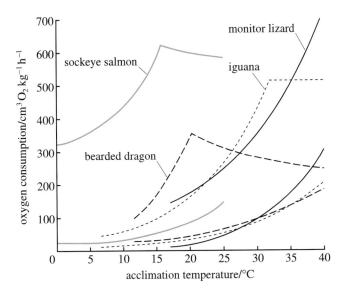

Figure 2.22 The relationship between oxygen consumption and acclimation temperature in the sockeye salmon (as in Figure 2.21) and representatives of three genera of lizards, the bearded dragon (*Amphibolurus barbatus*), the iguana (*Iguana iguana*) and the monitor lizard (*Varanus* sp.). For each species, the lower line shows 'basal' oxygen consumption, and the upper line shows aerobic capacity at a variety of acclimation temperatures.

metabolic scope that increases with temperature; it is distinguished among reptiles because it can maintain long periods of sustained activity. Figure 2.22 implies that much of this activity may be supported aerobically. In homeotherms, the story is different. Birds and mammals have a much higher resting oxygen consumption than that of poikilotherms. For example, the basal metabolic rates of birds and mammals are approximately five to ten times higher than the resting rates of similarly sized lizards at a body temperature of about 40 °C. The aerobic capacities of fish and reptiles are usually lower than the basal metabolic rates of similarly sized birds and mammals. As is evident from Table 2.2, not only is the basal metabolic rate of homeotherms higher than those of fish and reptiles, but the aerobic metabolic scope of mammals is usually greater.

■   What differences between poikilotherms and homeotherms do these figures highlight, with respect to energy needs and consumption of oxygen?

Most poikilotherms have much lower aerobic metabolic scopes than homeotherms but, for short periods, their burst activity can equal that of some homeotherms by relying on anaerobic mechanisms. An aquatic type of

Table 2.2 The minimum oxygen consumption (basal metabolic rate) and maximum oxygen consumption (aerobic capacity) in homeotherms and poikilotherms, comparing animals of equal mass.

	Salmon	Rat	Monitor lizard	Guinea pig
Body mass/g	350	350	700	700
Optimum temperature at which maximum O_2 consumption occurs/°C	15	30	40	30
Basal metabolic rate/ $cm^3 O_2 kg^{-1} h^{-1}$	50	800	100	700
Aerobic capacity/ $cm^3 O_2 kg^{-1} h^{-1}$	500	3 800	900	3 000

respiration ties the body temperature of most fish to that of the environment and the metabolic rate is usually comparatively low. Living in water allows neutrally buoyant fish to 'rest' economically after exertion and to utilize surplus oxygen as recovery oxygen. Lower vertebrates such as reptiles enjoy the benefit of a superior respiratory medium, but they are still tied to relatively inefficient anaerobic mechanisms that accumulate lactate, although large amounts of energy can be made available on demand. The ability of animals to increase maximum oxygen consumption (aerobic capacity) by a great amount evolved along with the development of homeothermy. Rather surprisingly, this condition is detectable in some exceptional fish (which we shall discuss in Chapter 3) but it is only fully developed in birds and mammals. These higher vertebrates have aerobic metabolic scopes that are many times greater than those of poikilothermic vertebrates, and this capacity for sustained aerobic metabolism has no doubt contributed to their great success.

2.4.2 Measuring swimming performance of fish

In studying performance of fish the following questions are often asked regarding swimming speeds:

■ (a)   What is the maximum speed?

   (b)   What is the maximum sustainable speed?

   (c)   What is the average speed normally used by fish in the wild?

Casual observation of fish leaping out of the water indicates that very high speeds are possible but obtaining clear measurements of the exact speed through the water is extraordinarily difficult. One indirect approach is to measure the height to which fish jump. Then by applying Newtonian mechanics, the take-off velocity from the water surface can be calculated. Salmon have been observed to jump 5 m to clear a waterfall. Such feats require a take-off velocity of $10\,\mathrm{m\,s^{-1}}$ or $12.5\,\mathrm{BL\,s^{-1}}$ for an 80 cm-long fish. We suspect this performance represents approximately the maximum burst speed of a salmon, but such jumps may be aided by water flow at the base of the waterfall. Scombroid fish (tunas and mackerel) are probably the fastest fish. A yellowfin tuna (*Thunnus albacares*) hooked on a line, with a recorder on the reel, was clocked at $20.7\,\mathrm{m\,s^{-1}}$ or $18\,\mathrm{BL\,s^{-1}}$. Video recordings of mackerel (*Scomber scombrus*) in a large enclosure revealed maximum burst speeds of $5.5\,\mathrm{m\,s^{-1}}$, which for a 30.5 cm-long fish is equivalent to $18\,\mathrm{BL\,s^{-1}}$. Such high-speed bursts generally last less than one minute and, after a burst, there is an enforced period of relative inactivity before burst swimming can recommence. This type of 'sprint' behaviour is linked with prey capture and/or pursuit from predators and, as in salmon, in the negotiation of obstacles and rapid currents. The body size of the fish has a major effect on the speed of burst swimming; small fish (10 cm) can achieve $30\,\mathrm{BL\,s^{-1}}$ (at 14 °C) with very high tail-beat frequencies. Even fairly poor swimmers like the carp and the wrasse are briefly able to achieve about $7\text{–}8\,\mathrm{BL\,s^{-1}}$.

Tag and recapture programmes have shown that a number of species of fish are capable of transoceanic journeys covering thousands of kilometres. One spiny dogfish tagged off the American west coast turned up over 8 700 km away near Japan. Two large bluefin tuna (*Thunnus thynnus*) crossed the Atlantic from Florida to Norway (6 700 km apart) in less than 120 days. Tagging of the longfin tuna (*Thunnus alalunga*) suggests that the fish migrate in schools on an extraordinary two-way trip from California to the mid-Pacific (or Japan) and

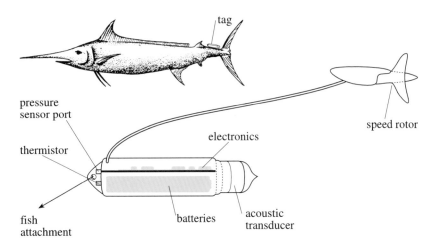

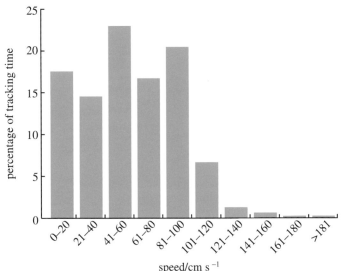

Figure 2.23 A speedometer transmitter tag (not to scale) as used to measure the swimming speed of blue marlin. The tag is attached to the back of the fish as shown. It transmits a coded acoustic signal to a boat carrying receiver equipment, enabling the exact speed of the fish to be recorded at any particular instant.

back again. One such school apparently covered 420 km in one day, equivalent to an average speed of 486 cm s^{-1} or 5.7 BL s^{-1} assuming a body length of about 85 cm. Other tagging studies indicate that average 'cruising' speeds of migrating fish are much lower. Such tagging studies, however, can only give an estimate of the average speed along a straight line between the release and recapture positions.

Fish can be directly tracked in the sea by tagging individuals with acoustic transmitters that emit an ultrasonic signal which can be picked up remotely by receiving equipment on board a boat. Kim Holland has tracked yellowfin tuna (*Thunnus albacares*) in this way off Hawaii. The fish swam continuously, generally near the surface at night, at 0–30 m depth, and deeper during the day, diving to 200 m. The average speed varied between 1.2 and 2.4 BL s^{-1}. The measurements, however, are hampered by the fact that the speed was calculated between hourly position fixes and might have missed convolutions in the path taken. Barbara Block and colleagues, therefore, attached a speedometer transmitter to a blue marlin (*Makaira nigricans*) (Figure 2.23). The transmitter encoded information on the rate of rotation of a propeller towed by the fish and thus gave precise information on swimming speed. Figure 2.24 shows the distribution of speeds observed. The highest speed recorded was 2.25 m s^{-1}, or approximately 1.5 BL s^{-1}. In fact, this species is capable of high-speed bursts, having been recorded to take baits trolled at 8 m s^{-1}.

Figure 2.24 The frequency distribution of speeds observed in the blue marlin.

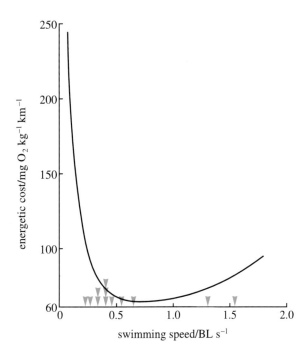

Figure 2.25   Swimming speeds (indicated by arrows) of Atlantic salmon (*Salmo salar*) tracked using acoustic tags during their migration at sea compared with the theoretical cost of transport (blue line) calculated from Brett's tunnel respirometer data. Note that most fish swim at a speed close to the theoretical optimum which is at the minimum of this curve.

Atlantic salmon (*Salmo salar*) have been tracked during their return migration to Scottish rivers from feeding grounds in the North Atlantic. The data showed that the fish swam continuously in a south-eastward direction at a speed of $0.65\,\text{BL s}^{-1}$. Thus, salmon, although capable of much higher speeds, use quite modest speeds for their transoceanic phase of migration. The reason can be seen in Figure 2.25, in which the cost of transport has been calculated by Gordon Smith of Aberdeen using the data of Brett (assuming that swimming metabolism is similar in Atlantic and Pacific salmon species). The speed for minimum cost of transport is at the minimum of the curve (as already shown in Table 2.1) and it seems that during their migration salmon are swimming continuously at close to the theoretical optimal speed.

Many species of fish, however, do not spend all their time swimming. Figure 2.26 shows the track of a pike (*Esox lucius*) in Loch Kinord near Aberdeen. Over a period of 90 hours it moved a total straight line distance of 750 m, a distance typical of many species of fish. The mean swimming speed along the track was $0.011\,\text{BL s}^{-1}$. Swimming was not continuous but was made up of short bursts with resting periods in between. The fish was patrolling a reed bed and feeding on young perch (*Perca fluviatilis*) that were emerging from the weeds at this time. The acoustic transmitter in this case telemetered the heart rate and muscle activity. Interference from the electromyograms (EMGs) gave an indication of the frequency of occurrence of bursts of swimming (Figure 2.27). Whenever the fish moved, as indicated by the EMGs, the heart rate increased but quickly fell to normal levels after the burst of activity, which indicated that

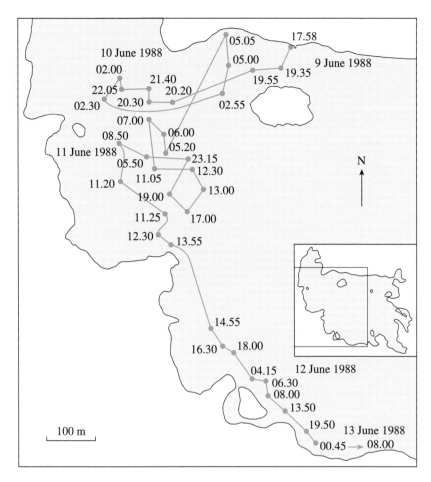

Figure 2.26 Track of a pike (*Esox lucius*) equipped with an acoustic heart beat transmitter in a freshwater loch (Scottish lake) near Aberdeen. The fish moved no more than 750 m in almost 4 days.

the fish did not incur a need for any recovery oxygen; during repayment of recovery oxygen we would expect the heart rate to remain high. The heart rate can be used as an approximate indicator of metabolic rate with 30 beats per minute as basal rate and 80 beats per minute as the aerobic capacity. Note the aerobic capacity was only reached for two minutes during the whole day. Uptake of recovery oxygen persisted for no more than 10 minutes. Most of the energy expenditure of the fish was associated with the digestion of the perch it was feeding on each day.

Studies on fish captured in trawls and on lines have caught the imagination of scientists who have been impressed by the swimming abilities and anaerobic capacity of fish. Telemetry studies in the field, however, show that most fish, even the continuous swimmers, spend most time at slow aerobic speeds. Most fish rarely exceed their aerobic limit. Most other animals probably do the same. We all know that human athletes can achieve phenomenal speeds but most of us rarely make use of our anaerobic sprint capacity! The small volume of red muscle in fish is therefore very important, as it is responsible for most of the swimming activity when the fish is likely to be cruising at its optimum speed.

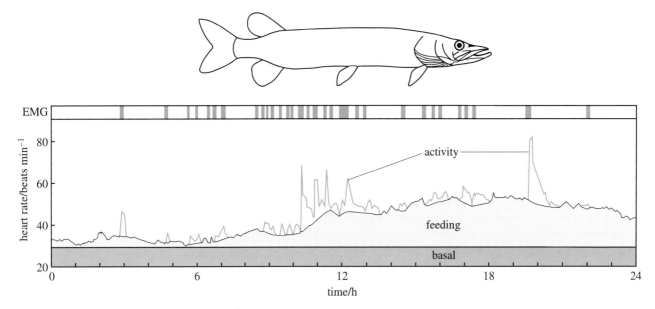

Figure 2.27   The heart rate and electromyogram record of the pike from Figure 2.26 during the third day. The heart rate has been divided into the basal rate (grey area at the bottom of the graph), a rate arising from feeding and digestion (the shaded blue area), and a rate arising from bursts of swimming activity. Note that the spikes indicating swimming activity correlate well with the EGM recording at the top of the graph.

Summary of Section 2.4

Many fish can maintain a steady cruising speed of approximately $0.1–6.0\,BL\,s^{-1}$ for prolonged periods, depending on the species. Some migrating fish swim more or less continuously over relatively long distances, as revealed by acoustic tags. Burst swimming is much faster (about $20\,BL\,s^{-1}$ in the yellowfin tuna) but can be maintained for only very brief periods, and recovery is often prolonged (up to 24 hours in captive mackerel). In sockeye salmon, oxygen consumption increases approximately 10-fold from a basal, resting level to swimming at $4\,BL\,s^{-1}$. At this speed, oxygen consumption is at a maximum level (termed the aerobic capacity) and faster swimming is sustained for short periods by increased anaerobic metabolism.

Temperature has a major effect on basal metabolism and aerobic capacity in fish, though differences between species are apparent. An approximate but sometimes unreliable measure of the ability of a fish to perform work is the aerobic metabolic scope, which also varies with temperature. More active fish tend to have higher aerobic metabolic scopes than less active fish species. In general, the aerobic capacities of many reptiles fall into approximately the same range as those of many fish, when measured at the same temperature. Bursts of intense activity in both reptiles and fish are fuelled almost exclusively by anaerobic mechanisms. Compared with reptiles, birds and mammals of about the same mass usually have a much higher basal metabolic rate and aerobic metabolic scope at the same body temperature. The combination of the air-breathing habit with homeothermy led to the development of a greatly improved ability to sustain activity exclusively by aerobic metabolism.

2.5 Conclusion

Fish swim with such apparent ease that it is hard for us to realize just how difficult it is to move rapidly through water. Unlike rigid structures such as submarines, which generate thrust with propellers, fish generate thrust by changing their shape as they move through water. Various fish have adopted unique methods of locomotion, using paired or unpaired fins to row, flap or undulate themselves along, but the great majority of fish propel themselves using a combination of two processes—the backward passage of transverse waves along the body and lateral movements of the caudal fin. In general, the fastest-swimming fish rely on the oscillation of a high-aspect-ratio caudal fin, which is attached to the body by a narrow caudal peduncle; slow-swimming fish undulate through the water like eels. The flexible method of thrust generation makes it impossible to apply directly hydrodynamic data from the performance of rigid bodies (such as submarines) to the analysis of fish swimming. Nonetheless, research into the hydrodynamics of fish swimming has made good progress over the last decade, particularly in the areas of obtaining kinematic and respirometric data from swimming fish set up in water tunnels and in working out suitable mathematical models of fish swimming. As a consequence, we can now make reasonable estimates of the power needed for swimming and of the efficiency of the process.

Objectives for Chapter 2

After completing Chapter 2 you should be able to:

2.1   Define and use, or recognize definitions and applications of, each of the **bold** terms.

2.2   Describe the arrangement of fish muscle and give reasons why myotomes have such complex shapes.

2.3   Draw a diagram illustrating the main forces acting on the body of a fish when the fish is (a) stationary and (b) moving forward.

2.4   Outline the concept of drag and describe the mechanisms used by fish to overcome drag.

2.5   Describe the morphological and functional differences between high- and low-aspect-ratio tails.

2.6   Outline the concept of hydrodynamic lift and describe the ways in which fish generate lift.

2.7   Explain what is meant by the aerobic capacity of a fish.

2.8   Describe some differences between poikilotherms and homeotherms with respect to aerobic metabolic capacities and scopes.

2.9   Give examples of the kinds of swimming speeds attainable by different species of fish, and the distances over which they travel.

Questions for Chapter 2

(*Answers to questions are at the end of the book.*)

Question 2.1 (Objectives 2.1, 2.2, 2.3, 2.4, 2.5 and 2.6)

Classify the following statements (a–i) as true or false and explain why.

(a)   The pectoral fins of all fish provide substantial hydrodynamic lift.

(b)   Bending of the body in fish is initiated when the myotomes on both sides of the spinal cord contract simultaneously.

(c)   The main locomotor muscles in tunas are confined to the peduncle, and they move the caudal fin from side to side.

(d)   In general, fish such as salmon and pike, which are highly manoeuvrable and can accelerate rapidly, have caudal and pectoral fins with a low AR.

(e)   In some fish, the backward-moving waves of muscular contraction are initially of relatively small amplitude and only the posterior portion of the body normally shows pronounced side-to-side movement.

(f)   In order to accelerate, a fish must generate a thrust force equal to and opposing the drag force.

(g)   When buoyancy is roughly equal to the weight of the fish, there is no tendency for the fish to rise or sink and the fish is said to be neutrally buoyant.

(h)   Fish that are denser than water, and do not utilize static lift, must maintain a minimum forward cruising speed to generate enough lift to prevent themselves from sinking.

(i)   The castor-oil fish has a complex skin that appears to be specialized for maintaining a turbulent boundary layer. Both the ctenoid scales and the sub-dermal spaces help prevent flow separation.

Question 2.2 (Objective 2.9)

Calculate the average swimming speed (in $BL\,s^{-1}$) of a 72 cm salmon that is observed to swim for 8 h and to cover a distance of 16 km. Make the rather unlikely assumptions that the fish is unaided by currents and swims at a constant speed.

Question 2.3 (Objective 2.9)

Classify the following swimming speeds as typical of burst or cruise swimming:

(a) $20\,BL\,s^{-1}$ in a 1 m yellowfin tuna;

(b) $6\,BL\,s^{-1}$ in a longfin tuna;

(c) $30\,BL\,s^{-1}$ in an unidentified 10 cm teleost;

(d) $4\,BL\,s^{-1}$ in a year-old sockeye salmon.

Question 2.4 (Objectives 2.7 and 2.8)

Classify the following statements (a–f) as true or false and explain why.

(a)   In natural conditions, swimming by salmon at a rate in excess of $4\,BL\,s^{-1}$ is likely to leave them exhausted for several hours.

(b)   Data for salmon (and bass) reveal that the basal metabolic rate of fish increases as the acclimation temperature increases.

(c)   Aerobic metabolic scope is a measure of the extent to which oxygen consumption can be increased by activity; in fish this scope is a function of temperature.

(d)   The duration of burst swimming is not likely to be influenced by the amount of stored glycogen in the muscle.

(e)   Air-breathing poikilotherms have a much greater aerobic metabolic scope than water-breathing fish of comparable size.

(f)   Compared with birds and mammals, reptiles and fish generally place a greater reliance on anaerobic metabolism to fuel intense activity.

CHAPTER 3 SWIMMING: MUSCLES AND MOVEMENT

Prepared for the Course Team by Mandy Dyson

3.1 Introduction

Now that you know something about the mechanics and energetics of it, we can look at the arrangement of the muscles that power locomotion. You know already that swimming in most fish involves sustained 'cruising' at low speeds and infrequent bursts of intense activity. Fish can, of course, swim at all speeds up to their maximum. When the swimming speed doubles, the drag on the body increases so markedly that the force the muscles produce has to increase eight fold. This great variation in the power output required from the trunk musculature poses formidable mechanical problems. The solution is that the locomotory musculature of most fish is divided into two distinct components that differ in major ways with respect to both structure and function. As much as 90% of fish muscle consists of 'white' fibres (the familiar fish fillet of culinary delight!), which has a relatively meagre blood supply. In contrast, the relatively small strips of 'red' muscle are well supplied with capillaries and, in many fish, this red muscle forms narrow superficial sheets on the lateral flanks (Figure 3.1a). However, the total volume occupied by red fibres varies between different fish species, from about 1% of the total lateral muscle volume in the cod, to 14% in the herring. The first part of this chapter examines the differences in arrangement and physiology of these two muscle types and relates these to differences in how the muscles are used to power swimming movements. In the second part of the chapter we look at a unique feature of some fish that enables them to maintain body temperature above ambient.

Figure 3.1 (a) Cross-section of a typical fish body showing the large mass of white muscle and the superficial layers of red muscle. (b) Idealized vertical sections through single muscle fibres. (c) Idealized cross-sections through groups of muscle fibres. The top and bottom diagrams in (b) and (c) illustrate the different types of innervation pattern found in white muscle fibres, while the middle diagrams illustrate the innervation pattern found in red muscle fibres.

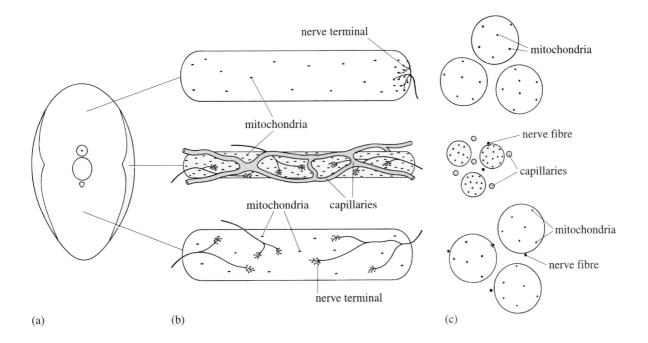

(a)　　　(b)　　　(c)

3.2 Muscle physiology

The geometric arrangements of the red and white muscle fibres in the myotomes of fish are very different. Red muscle fibres (and in some fish the superficial layers of white muscle fibres) are oriented parallel to the longitudinal axis of the fish, whereas the deeper layers of white fibres are arranged in a complex helical pattern (see Figure 2.7). However, in addition to the differences in their arrangement, red and white muscle fibres differ substantially both in their physiology and in their biochemistry.

The following list of items (1–4) presents some of the features of the two muscle types: from each item you should try to deduce something about how each type of muscle might *function*. To help you, look back at Figure 3.1, which shows diagramatically the appearance of both types of muscle fibre in vertical section along the length of the fibre (b) and in cross-section (c).

1   Some of the earliest experiments involved inserting electrodes into the trunk musculature of the dogfish and recording the electrical activity associated with different types of movement. First, the tip of the recording electrode was placed within the superficial red muscle sheet. When the fish was swimming slowly and steadily, regular bursts of electrical activity indicated periodic contraction of the muscle fibres. When the electrode was inserted into the main bulk of white muscle, no electrical activity was apparent as long as the fish was swimming steadily. However, once the fish was provoked to swim in a vigorous burst, the white musculature displayed bursts of electrical activity.

2   Fish red muscle is rich in mitochondria (see Figures 3.1b and 3.2a). If the density of mitochondria is expressed as a percentage of the total fibre volume, many teleosts have values for their red muscle that exceed 30%—only slightly less than the mitochondrial density in the heart (ventricular) muscle of birds and mammals.

3   Teleost white muscle is poorly vascularized (Figure 3.1b). In some species, nearly half of the white muscle fibres have no associated capillaries and most of the remainder have only a single adjacent capillary. Red muscle is heavily vascularized—typically there are about five or six capillaries adjacent to each fibre. How much oxygen is available to different muscle types is also determined by myoglobin content and by fibre size—white fibres have a lower concentration of myoglobin than red fibres and are of greater diameter.

4   During 'burst' swimming there is an extremely rapid breakdown of phosphocreatine stores in white muscle. For activity lasting more than a few tailbeats, glycogen is also mobilized. For example, in the trout, about one half of the glycogen of white muscle is utilized in 15 seconds of intense activity All the lactic acid formed during burst activity can be accounted for by glycogen breakdown.

■   From points 1–4, what can you conclude about the respective functions of white and red fish muscle?

On this evidence it seem that red muscle is used mainly for sustained, steady swimming (see item 1) and that metabolic energy for this is derived mainly from aerobic mechanisms (see item 2). Indeed red muscle is strikingly well adapted for aerobic metabolism, with a high mitochondrial density, a high level of vascularization, and substantial myoglobin content (see item 3).

White muscle functions as an 'emergency power pack'—active only during brief, intense bouts of burst swimming when the power demand from the musculature is greatest. Escape responses and predation fast starts often involve only a few tailbeats at, or close to, maximum speed. Because it is of such short duration, the fuel for this kind of behaviour is mostly phosphocreatine (PCr) (see item 4) which is present at a concentration of around $30\,mmol\,kg^{-1}$ in the white muscle. White muscle contains high concentrations of the enzyme creatine phosphokinase (CPK) which hydrolyses PCr to ATP. Because only one enzyme step is involved, ATP is produced very quickly which, together with the rapid appearance of lactate and utilization of glycogen after a few tailbeats, suggests that white muscle is primarily an anaerobic tissue. (Indeed, you should recall that its blood supply is relatively sparse (item 3) and perhaps just sufficient for maintenance of the tissue and for slow recovery after exertion.)

■   The advantage of anaerobic pathways is that energy is supplied rapidly. What is a major disadvantage of such pathways?

Although anaerobic pathways supply energy more rapidly, they have an important disadvantage—lactic acid must be excreted or has to be oxidized *in situ* before muscle can be activated again. It can take up to 24 hours to remove lactic acid after an all-out burst of activity.

There are some interesting biochemical differences between red and white muscle fibres.

■   In which types of fibres would you expect:
(a)   high activities of creatine phosphokinase;
(b)   an active lactate dehydrogenase, which channels pyruvate into lactate;
(c)   a high content of tricarboxylic acid (TCA) cycle enzymes;
(d)   a greater capacity to consume oxygen?

In white muscle, CPK hydrolyses PCr to ATP (a). White muscle is geared primarily for anaerobic metabolism, and the rapid production of lactate is achieved by active lactate dehydrogenase (b). Red muscle has a high potential for aerobic metabolism (remember its high mitochondrial density), which is linked with a vigorous TCA cycle and high overall O_2 consumption (c and d).

The different properties of red and white muscle fibres result in part from the presence of different isoforms of the contractile proteins and metabolic enzymes, which have distinct functional characteristics. For example, myosin occurs in several different isoforms which determine, to a large extent, how fast a muscle can contract. Red muscle fibres contain 'slow' isoforms of myosin which result in slower shortening velocities than those of white muscle fibres. Red and white muscle fibres also differ with respect to the numbers of ion channels, membrane pumps and cellular organelles that are present. In white muscle, the myofibrils are more densely packed than in red muscle, which increases the potential power output. Compared with red muscle, relatively little of the cross-sectional area is occupied by mitochondria or capillaries (Figure 3.1c). A short twitch contraction time is ensured by having a well-developed sarcoplasmic reticulum (SR) and high SR Ca^{2+}-ATPase activity, a fast shortening velocity (due to the presence of 'fast' isoforms of myosin) and high concentrations of cytoplasmic Ca^{2+}-binding proteins called parvalbumins. These features enable white muscle fibres to develop a great deal of force rapidly and to contract at high frequency during burst swimming. Generating ATP by anaerobic glycolysis is relatively inefficient in energetic terms (net ATP per mol glucose is only a fraction of that generated through the aerobic pathway), but this price is acceptable if it means that the system can ensure high-speed swimming that is largely independent of the supply of oxygen (except during recovery from exercise).

By contrast, red muscle is designed for economy. The myofibrils occupy only about 40–60% of the total volume of the muscle (compared with 80–90% in white) and, as you know, aerobic metabolism is supported by the abundant capillary supply and high mitochondrial content. There is a close correlation between the degree of vascularization, the mitochondrial content and the aerobic metabolic scope (Section 2.4.1) of different fish. For example, the European anchovy (*Engraulis encrasicolus*) is a filter feeder subject to high drag forces during continuous swimming; a high sustained power output from red muscle by aerobic means is essential. Mitochondria in the red muscle of this species are particularly numerous and have a complex structure (Figure 3.2a).

There is general agreement that in fish, the bulk of muscle is made up of slow red and fast white fibres. However, two additional types of fibre have been found. In some species, intermediate pink fibres are situated as a distinct layer between the red and white fibres. The contractile and metabolic properties of the pink fibres are intermediate to those of red and white muscle fibres. Electromyographical recordings of muscle activity have shown that as swimming speed increases there is a sequential activation of red, then pink and finally white muscle fibres.

(a)

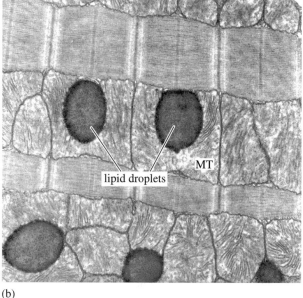

(b)

Figure 3.2   (a) An electron micrograph of an anchovy red muscle fibre in longitudinal section. Note the abundant mitochondria (MT). (b) An electron micrograph of a mackerel red muscle fibre in longitudinal section. Note the close relationship between the lipid droplets (black) and surrounding mitochondria.

A fourth type of fibre is found in many bottom-living species, including the dogfish and flatfish (e.g. plaice). In these fish, a layer of pale muscle fibres is situated between the skin and the red muscle layer. These fibres have relatively few mitochondria and myofibrils, a low concentration of myoglobin and a poorly developed SR. They are thought to play a mainly postural role, functioning to bend the body and raise the head above the sea bed.

White and red muscle are often referred to as 'fast' and 'slow' muscle, respectively. This classification is based largely on differences in the maximum shortening velocity (v_{max}) between the two muscle types. The v_{max} of white fibres is two to four times higher than that of red muscle fibres. White muscle fibres are activated by action potentials, and they respond to a stimulus with a fast twitch which is 25–50% shorter in duration than that observed in red muscle. The electrophysiological properties of red muscle fibres have only been examined in a very few species. These studies have shown that red muscle fibres respond to a single stimulus with a slow twitch and that the majority are also activated by action potentials. Red muscle fibres can therefore be compared to the slow fibres found in other vertebrates which also have a low contraction velocity. However, they differ from the 'true' slow fibres of vertebrates which are activated by junction potentials and produce a slow graded contraction on multiple stimulation.

3.2.1 Muscle innervation

Innervation of fish muscle differs from the general pattern found in other vertebrate muscles which usually have either tonic or twitch fibres. The tonic fibres are not able to conduct action potentials, and contract slowly after a series of stimuli. Twitch fibres conduct action potentials and produce a quick twitch contraction after one stimulus. Fish muscle fibres differ from this simple dichotomy. Red muscle fibres are slow but, in contrast to other vertebrate slow fibres, react to a single stimulus with a twitch. This twitch response is facilitated by **polyneuronal multiple innervation**, where a high density of nerve terminals is dispersed over the fibre surface (see centre diagram in Figure 3.1b).

Innervation divides fast white twitch fibres into two types: **focally innervated** fibres, where the branches of the axon terminate on the muscle fibre as a structure called the **motor end plate**, which in focal innervation is confined to the terminal part of the fibre (see top diagram in Figure 3.1b); and **multiply innervated** fibres which have similar innervation to that of red fibres (see bottom diagram in Figure 3.1b). For example, on average, each fast fibre in the cod has between 15 and 28 motor end plates derived from a large number of different axons. A single axon may branch repeatedly near the muscle to form a number of motor end plates dispersed over the same fibre. More usually a branching axon gives rise to numerous motor end plates that innervate several adjacent fibres (see Figure 3.3). Until recently, the generally accepted idea was that in elasmobranchs, lungfish and more primitive groups of teleosts, white muscle fibres were focally innervated. In contrast, it was thought that in the majority of more recent teleost orders, white fast fibres were multiply innervated. It is now apparent that this dichotomy in the innervation of white fibres between primitive and advanced teleosts is no longer strictly valid. The ancestral pattern has been found in the brown bullhead, an advanced teleost, while in a closely related catfish, the multiple (advanced) pattern is displayed.

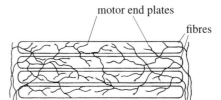

motor end plates

fibres

Figure 3.3   Multiple innervation in the white fibres of an advanced teleost.

■   What is the functional significance of multiple innervation in fish?

Electromyographical recordings of muscle activity have been conducted on some advanced teleost species (particularly the brook trout, *Salvelinus fontinalis*) which have a multiple pattern of innervation in the white muscle. Electrodes were placed at two locations, one within the red muscle and the other within the white, in a trout trained to swim in a swimming chamber (see Figure 3.4). The recorded electrical activity at both sites at two different swimming speeds is shown in the lower half of Figure 3.4. At steady swimming of $1\,BL\,s^{-1}$, potentials are recorded only from the red muscle (see blue trace), except when the fish changes its position in the swimming chamber (see arrowed trace). When the swimming speed increases to $3\,BL\,s^{-1}$, the red muscle potentials increase in frequency and amplitude (see blue trace). However, what is particularly striking is the onset of regular electrical activity in the white muscle, even though the swimming speed is well below the burst maximum and can be maintained continuously for at least three weeks. This situation is in contrast to the dogfish and the herring, both of which have focally innervated fast fibres that are probably used exclusively for burst swimming. So the brook trout recruits multiply innervated white fibres not just for burst swimming but for sustainable speeds as well. Although, in general, teleost white muscle is poorly vascularized, in many advanced teleosts, such as the trout, there are significant numbers of mitochondria and a fairly extensive capillary blood supply in the white muscle, so aerobic metabolism may be more prominent. Multiple innervation in teleosts may therefore ensure great flexibility in the development of power by the musculature because the full activation of each muscle fibre probably requires simultaneous activity in a number of different motor neurons. What is certain is that we should no longer regard fish white and red muscle as completely distinct locomotor systems utilizing different biochemical processes; there is considerable overlap in the function of red and white muscle systems.

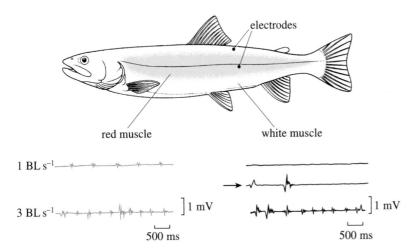

Figure 3.4   The recruitment of fibres in the brook trout during swimming. Electrodes are inserted into the red and white muscle as indicated. The top traces show electromyograms (EMGs) recorded in the red and white muscle regions during sustained swimming at $1\,BL\,s^{-1}$. The bottom traces show EMGs at a steady swimming speed of $3\,BL\,s^{-1}$. The arrowed trace is the EMG recorded when the fish changes its position in the swimming chamber.

We should consider the fate of lactate produced in the white muscle of most fish. In mammals, most lactate (as much as 80%) is immediately released into the blood and rapidly oxidized during recovery by being shunted into the TCA cycle (where it is oxidized eventually to CO_2 and water). In addition, lactate is a gluconeogenic substrate, that is, it is converted into glucose, by a process that indirectly requires oxygen.In fish, lactate accumulates during burst swimming and is probably held in white muscle, which may explain in part why burst swimming can only be of very short duration (the dwindling amounts of stored glycogen probably exert the major influence). During the recovery phase, most of the accumulated lactate is oxidized using recovery oxygen. As in mammals, lactate may also be a gluconeogenic substrate for fish.

■   If, in some fish, the white muscle is active anaerobically during sustained, steady swimming, how might a fish avoid a large build-up of lactate which might limit the duration of swimming?

If ^{14}C-lactate is supplied to fish tissue, the gills, liver, red muscle and kidney are able to oxidize it. One suggestion has been that fish export some lactate from the white muscle to peripheral sites for oxidation, especially to the red muscles where O_2 supply might be sustained. Moreover, some workers believed that glucose (stored as glycogen) in the red fibres could be transferred to white fibres, and that red fibres had an important gluconeogenic role, i.e. they might synthesize glucose from imported lactate. However, the idea that red muscle metabolizes lactate is no longer widely accepted. It is now believed that lactate is converted into glucose within white muscle, rather than being exported. This is certainly likely to happen during recovery from burst swimming, and we have noted already that, in some species, white muscle has appreciable aerobic potential. It is significant too that in red muscle, the key enzymes of gluconeogenesis, for example phosphoenolpyruvate (PEP) carboxykinase, are absent, or their activity is very slight.

Up to now we have talked exclusively of carbohydrate metabolism in fish muscle, but proteins and fats are also important metabolic fuels. Muscle proteins in fish appear to have a key role during starvation, which may be a fairly common occurrence in the wild. Fish muscle proteins are freely mobilized during starvation, and often in preference to stores of carbohydrate and lipid. Fish may therefore have unique storage proteins that can be broken down on demand; the amino acids released are probably converted into glucose via gluconeogenic pathways in the liver. Mammals store fat as adipose tissue but although some teleosts have adipose tissue, in many fish fat stores are dispersed through the major body organs. The fat content of red muscle may be relatively high (see Figure 3.2b). For this type of muscle, the principal fuels are fatty acids (in teleosts) and ketone bodies (in elasmobranchs). Triglyceride breakdown (lipolysis) releases free fatty acids (a process stimulated in fish by hormones, e.g. noradrenalin). In mammals, oxidation of free fatty acids is a major energy-yielding process. The process has not yet been studied in fish but fat oxidation is known to be important during the steady swimming of prolonged migration. Oil (and proteins) in the muscles of salmon become depleted during upstream migration of the adult.

3.2.2 Work from muscles

You already know that the white muscle fibres of teleosts are not orientated parallel to the body axis (as red fibres are) but run obliquely in a complex helical way (Figure 3.5a).

■   How does this complex arrangement facilitate the function of white muscle in powering the short bursts of fast swimming that are usually associated with the pursuit of prey or escape from predators?

One major consequence is that as the body of the fish undulates through the water, white fibres shorten over a distance that is approximately equal for all fibres regardless of their position relative to the vertebral column (Section 2.2). Another important consequence of this arrangement was found by Dr Larry Rome and co-workers at the University of Pennsylvania. They measured the sarcomere length of muscle fibres in carp when they were bent to different body curvatures (Figure 3.5b) and found that for a given curvature of the body, the red fibres had to shorten four times as much as the white fibres. In other words, the white fibres have a four-fold higher gearing ratio due to their complex helical arrangement. The gearing ratio sets the velocity at which the fibres must shorten to produce a movement. For instance, if red muscle had to power an escape response, it would need to shorten at a rate of 20 lengths s^{-1}, i.e. five times faster than its v_{max} of 4 lengths s^{-1}. However, due to its helical arrangement, white muscle can power this movement while shortening at a rate of 5 lengths s^{-1}, which is well below its v_{max}.

Differences in fibre arrangement also relate to the amount of force generated by the two fibre types under fast and sustained swimming conditions.

The highest force produced by muscle occurs when the length of the sarcomeres is approximately twice the length of the thin filaments within the sarcomere or, in other words, when the portions of thick filaments that bear crossbridges overlap to the greatest extent with the thin filaments. The curve in Figure 3.5c describes the isometric force at a range of sarcomere lengths for frog muscle. Since the lengths of the thick and thin filaments in red and white muscles of the carp are similar to those of frog muscle, we can use the relationship between sarcomere length and force for frog muscles, for the red and white muscles of carp. Rome and colleagues found that during sustained swimming in the carp, the sarcomere lengths of superficial red muscles vary between 1.9 and 2.2 µm. Figure 3.5c shows that over this range (indicated by the arrowed line marked red muscle), the force generated by the red muscle fibres is greater than 96% of its maximum value. At high swimming speeds and during vigorous left-right escape movements the deep white muscle takes over from the red. The sarcomere lengths of white muscle are estimated to vary between 1.7 and 2.2 µm (indicated by the arrowed line marked white muscle) and the isometric tension at these lengths is within 85% of the maximum. Remember that red muscle fibres, because they are oriented parallel to the body axis, would have to shorten approximately four times as much as white fibres for the same body curvature. Research has shown that if red muscle was used during escape responses, it would have to shorten to about 1.5 µm to achieve the same degree of body curvature. At this length, the red muscle would generate only 50% of its maximum isometric force (shown by the dashed black line in Figure 3.5c). If white muscle fibres were arranged parallel to the body axis, as red fibres are,

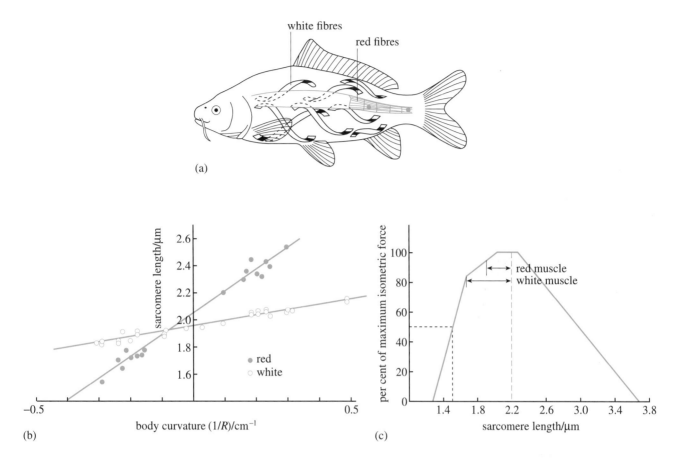

Figure 3.5 (a) The arrangement of superficial red fibres and deeper white fibres in the carp. (b) The relative gearing of the red and white muscle. In the middle of the fish, sarcomere length (SL) is a function of body curvature, 1/R, where R is the radius of curvature of the backbone. The slope for the red muscle (1.69) is much greater than that for the white fibres (0.39). This means that a given SL change in white muscle causes a much greater bending of the fish than the same SL change in red muscle. (c) Isometric force (as % of maximum) generated by white and red muscle at different sarcomere lengths.

they would have to shorten significantly more to generate the kinds of body curvature associated with fast escape movements and, like red muscle, would only generate about 50% of their maximum force. The helical arrangement therefore allows white fibres to generate maximum force at body curvatures that are characteristic of movements associated with burst activity by fish.

If red and white muscle are used to power sustained and burst swimming, respectively, then they must operate most effectively at different tailbeat frequencies. During slow sustained swimming, the tail moves through one complete cycle less frequently than when the fish rapidly accelerates to avoid predation or to pursue prey. Red and white muscle fibres therefore produce their maximum power output at different cycle (or tailbeat) frequencies. Altringham and Johnstone tested red and white intact fibres of the bullrout (*Myoxocephalus scorpius*) under conditions simulating red and white muscle activity in fish swimming at different speeds. They found that red fibres developed their maximum power of 5–8 W kg^{-1} wet muscle mass at a tailbeat frequency of 2 Hz,

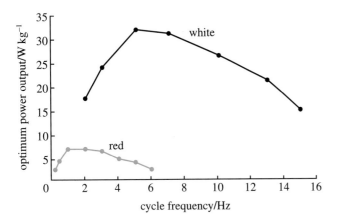

Figure 3.6   The optimum power output plotted against cycle (tailbeat) frequency for representative red (slow) and white (fast) fibre preparations.

whereas white fibres produced their maximum power of 25–30 W kg^{-1} at tailbeat frequencies of 5–8 Hz. The power output of red muscle fibres was negligible relative to that of white fibres at high frequencies (Figure 3.6). In other words, white muscle fibres produce more power at high tailbeat frequencies than do slow red fibres. Above 8 Hz, the twitch kinetics and shortening velocity of red fibres are too slow to generate net positive work. This property provides one explanation of why muscle fibre types with different contraction speeds are required for fish to swim over a wide range of speeds.

3.2.3 Muscle action during swimming

You already know that to swim at a steady speed, a fish must produce power, and that this power is generated by myotomal muscle on both sides of the body. Most fish swim by the sequential activation of myotomes on alternate sides of the body which can be detected by EMG running from head to tail. This, together with the arrangement of the myosepta and the interaction between the fish's body and the reactive forces from the water in which it moves, produces a wave of lateral bending which also travels caudally, from head to tail. During steady swimming, the muscle fibres lengthen and shorten rhythmically. The power generated by muscle contraction is converted into thrust, either along the length of the fish, or at the tail, depending on the swimming mode.

For many years, electromyography, in conjunction with kinematic analysis of body shape changes, has been used to address the problem of how fish use their muscles to swim. More recently, the information derived from these studies has been used on isolated muscle fibres to simulate, *in vitro*, the *in vivo* operating conditions, yielding previously unobtainable information. Current theory is that there is a gradual change in muscle function along the length of the fish. Specifically, the anterior musculature generates most of the power and the posterior musculature only transmits the force to the tail. By analogy then, the anterior muscle is the 'motor', the posterior muscle is the 'drive shaft' and the tail is the 'propeller'. The reason why there is a shift in muscle function along the length of the fish is because the waves of muscle activation, alternating from left to right sides, travel faster than those of body curvature, which leads to systematic phase differences between muscle length change (strain cycle) and muscle activation (activation cycle) along the body. Muscle activation in myotomes located towards the head (rostral region) occurs when the muscle fibres are shortening, producing net positive work over the entire tailbeat cycle. In the middle of the fish, muscle fibres are active during both shortening and lengthening, such that the amounts of positive and negative work almost cancel each other out. In contrast, the muscle fibres towards the tail (caudal region) develop force mainly while being stretched. This greatly stiffens the muscle and results in the production of net negative work.

■ How might these muscles, operating in such different ways, act together to contribute to the power required for the generation of thrust at the caudal fin?

The instantaneous power output of muscles at three positions on the body of a fish (at 0.35, 0.5 and 0.65 BL) is shown in Figure 3.7. You can see from the figure that at the instant that the rostral muscle (at 0.35 BL) generates maximum power, the activated caudal myotomes reach maximum, or close to maximum force/stiffness while still lengthening (negative work). The stretching of active muscle serves to increase the force generated during the shortening phase—since work is force multiplied by distance moved, muscle performs more work after a prestretch than without it—and the highest instantaneous power output occurs after prestretch of the caudal muscle. Negative work is performed at both 0.5 BL and 0.65 BL as power increases at 0.35 BL. As power begins to decline at 0.35 BL, power output at 0.5 BL becomes positive and rises. Force at 0.65 BL remains high, and the muscle continues to perform negative work as a power transmitter until just before power at 0.5 BL peaks. Only then does muscle at 0.65 BL perform positive work, with peak positive power at this location occurring when the power output at 0.5 BL falls towards 50% of maximum positive power. The rostral muscle therefore acts primarily as a power generator, and this power is transmitted towards the tail blade by the stiffened myotomes (which resist stretch) placed more caudally. Only when the power output of the rostral muscle declines does the caudal muscle in turn act as a power generator.

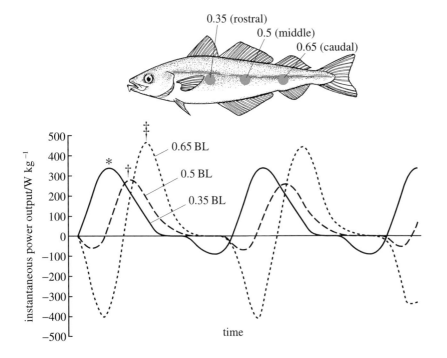

Figure 3.7 The instantaneous power curves for the saithe (*Pollachius virens*) for muscle at three points along the body, over two tailbeats. The strain (muscle length change) and stimulation parameters simulated those *in vivo* during steady swimming. Power is generated as a caudally travelling wave. Muscle at all locations has both positive and negative work phases, with the relative magnitude of the negative work phase increasing towards the tail. Negative work production by the more caudal myotomes coincides with the power-generating phase in the rostral myotomes. *, † and ‡ = peak power output at 0.35, 0.5 and 0.65 BL, respectively.

The caudal fibres therefore function in the transmission of power from the rostral myotomes to the tail blade during the first part of the tailbeat cycle. Although tendons could provide a similar function to that of caudal muscle fibres (as they do in tunas), having muscle fibres at the caudal peduncle (Figure 2.1) is far more versatile and greatly improves manoeuvring performance.

Summary of Section 3.2

Most of the muscle of fish consists of white (or fast) fibres, the structure of which is well suited to produce the explosive bursts of muscular power that are necessary for movement at high speed through water. Fish have variable amounts of red (slow) muscle, which often forms a thin superficial strip along the flank. Its metabolism is primarily aerobic and lipid is a major fuel for it. Red muscle has a high mitochondrial density and a rich capillary network, features that are particularly apparent in fish such as the European anchovy (*Engraulis encrasicolus*) which has a high aerobic metabolic scope. Red fibres are slow, but virtually inexhaustible and their metabolism is aerobic. By contrast, white muscle has a high creatine phosphokinase activity for hydrolysis of phosphocreatine to ATP, contains large amounts of glycogen and has a high anaerobic potential; its activity during burst swimming is therefore largely independent of the supply of oxygen. A large demand for glucose is reflected in the relatively high activities of the enzymes that break down glycogen (e.g. phosphorylase).

In contrast to other vertebrate slow fibres, fish red fibres react to a single stimulus because of the high density of nerve terminals on the fibres. White fibres are either focally or multiply innervated. In the dogfish, for example, white muscle is innervated at one end of the fibre and is recruited only during burst swimming. In other species, for example, the trout, white muscle has multiple innervation and is active at modest, sustainable cruising speeds, as well as during burst swimming. Multiple innervation may enable a graded and more flexible pattern of muscle recruitment.

The various muscle fibre types are distinguished by their possession of different isoforms of the contractile proteins with distinct functional properties, and by differences in the numbers of myofibrils, mitochondria, ion pumps and channels, and the amount of sarcoplasmic reticulum. The contractile properties of the different muscle fibre types are 'tuned' to the locomotory frequencies over which they are recruited. The average power output of white muscle fibres is around four times greater than that of red muscle fibres, and is produced at higher frequencies. During continuous swimming the red and superficial white muscle fibres undergo cyclic length changes. The waves of lateral undulations running from head to tail travel more slowly than the wave of muscle contraction producing them, reflecting the interaction of the body with reactive forces from the water. This results in systematic differences in the timing of activation in relation to the muscle length cycle at different points along the body. The muscle fibres in the rostral and middle myotomes function entirely as power generators and are active during shortening. In contrast, muscle fibres towards the caudal peduncle are initially active during lengthening, increasing their stiffness and tensile stress and enabling them to function in the transmission of power from the anterior of the fish to the tail blade.

3.3 Warm-bodied fish

The tunas and related species make up a relatively small part of the family Scombridae (which also includes the bonitos and mackerel). Tunas are important fish in both a commercial and a physiological sense. Among the teleost fish, they are some of the largest in size and the swiftest swimmers. Tunas can be thought of as the 'gas guzzlers' of the fish world: rapid swimming in large fish is very expensive in metabolic terms. It is no easy task to measure the metabolic rate of such large, active fish, but we do know that their oxygen consumption is very high; in the skipjack tuna swimming at $2\,BL\,s^{-1}$, oxygen uptake is $422\,cm^3\,O_2\,kg^{-1}\,h^{-1}$ compared with $140–300\,cm^3\,O_2\,kg^{-1}\,h^{-1}$ in a range of eight 'non-tuna' species. Skipjack tuna are usually captured at sea after a prolonged chase at high speeds, and their oxygen uptake may then rise to a value of $910\,cm^3\,O_2\,kg^{-1}\,h^{-1}$. This rate implies that at least some tunas have an extremely large aerobic metabolic scope, higher indeed than that recorded for any other fish, amphibian or reptile. It seems that tunas are not geared to burst swimming—their performance resembles that of middle-distance runners rather than sprinters. They are able to sustain higher swimming speeds than most other teleosts and possess a number of specializations for this increased swimming performance. Morphological adaptations include a streamlined body shape to reduce drag, fin grooves to increase streamlining, a high-aspect-ratio tail with a narrow caudal peduncle and finlets along the trailing edges of the body.

Skipjack tuna about 40–50 cm long can swim at speeds of about $10\,BL\,s^{-1}$ for at least one hour, a performance well beyond that of most other fish species of this size, in which high-speed swimming usually terminates after a few minutes. Swimming of this speed and duration is feasible only when linked with a very high oxygen consumption, so the key question is: what feature of tuna biology enables them to display a metabolic rate more than twice that of any other fish?

Part of the answer lies in the fact that some of the larger tunas and some sharks are able to maintain their muscle temperature significantly above ambient temperature because they have vascular arrangements that reduce the extent of heat loss from certain areas of the body to the environment. This arrangement is likely to have many benefits but the most direct appears to be that increased muscle temperature can elevate the metabolic rate of tunas to near mammalian levels, and so maximize sustained swimming speeds.

This property of tunas has been known since 1835, when the physician Davy, who sailed with Darwin on the Beagle, reported that skipjack tuna were always warmer than the water in which they were caught. But measuring temperatures in large active fish was not easy using mercury thermometers, and reliable field measurements had to await work by Americans in the 1970s who used small electronic thermometers to record temperatures within the swimming muscles of bluefin tuna.

■ Figure 3.8 shows muscle temperatures for both bluefin and skipjack tuna captured at a variety of locations with different surface-water temperatures. It is clear that neithet species is a true poikilotherm because in both fish muscle temperature is normally at least 5 °C above water temperature. What is the most striking difference between these two species?

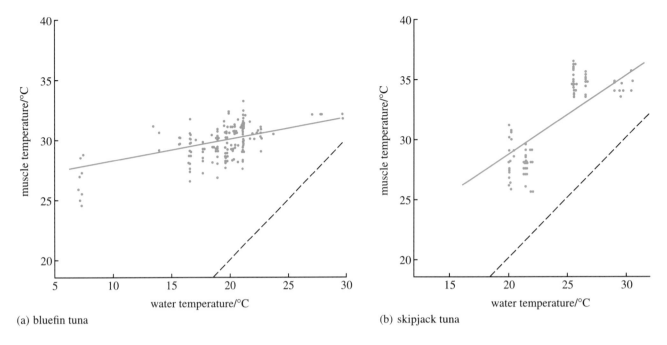

(a) bluefin tuna

(b) skipjack tuna

Figure 3.8   The maximum recorded temperatures in red muscle of (a) bluefin tuna (*Thunnus thynnus*), and (b) skipjack tuna (*Euthynnus affinis)* caught in the wild at a variety of water temperatures. In each case, the dashed line (known as the isothermal line) shows the relationship between muscle and water temperatures that one would predict of a perfect conformer, i.e. a poikilotherm.

The muscle temperature of skipjacks is raised by a relatively fixed amount (about 5 °C) above ambient, irrespective of the prevailing water temperature (for convenience, the difference between muscle and water temperature is called the excess). These observations imply that skipjack tuna muscle generates and retains a good deal of metabolic heat (i.e. skipjack tuna are endotherms). However, in the bluefin tuna, the difference between muscle and ambient temperature (the excess) is greater in fish from cold water than from warm water, suggesting that bluefin tunas approach true homeothermy—they may vary the degree to which heat is conserved (conserving or generating more heat in cold water) and so keep body temperature relatively stable.

■   What is the source of the metabolic heat?

Tunas have relatively large amounts of red muscle, much of which is located internally (Figure 3.9), and this tissue is highly vascularized, with high concentrations of mitochondrial enzymes typical of aerobic metabolism (e.g. cytochrome oxidase). A tissue that is so metabolically active is likely to be the primary site of heat production, but the mass of red muscle is at most, only one-third that of white. Tuna white muscle has unusually large amounts of glycogen and the highest recorded lactate dehydrogenase (LDH) activity in nature. This immense anaerobic capacity means that white muscle can accumulate about 100 µmol of lactate per gram wet weight of tissue after a 10-minute burst at about 70 km h^{-1}. It has been calculated that if all the glycogen stored in the white muscle was instantaneously metabolized anaerobically to lactate and all the chemical energy liberated as heat, muscle temperatures would be raised by just 2.5 °C. Recorded excess temperatures can approach 10 °C, so we have to look to red muscle as the primary site of heat production. However, we should not dismiss white muscle altogether. Suspensions of white muscle tissue consume oxygen at 15% of the rate of red muscle (which may be linked to the need to restore white-muscle glycogen levels after depletion). This observation raises at least two intriguing points: (i) white muscle may produce some heat, particularly at higher cruising speeds and burst speeds, and (ii) a powerful anaerobic system is located in a tissue that also has a marked aerobic potential and the activity of these two types of metabolism must therefore be tightly integrated, although we are unsure of the biochemical mechanisms involved.

3.3.1 Counter-current heat exchangers

In a 'conventional' fish the dorsal aorta forms the main blood supply to the body and runs just beneath the vertebral column, close to the posterior cardinal vein. Branches of both vessels form segmental arteries and veins leading to and from the surrounding musculature. Any metabolic heat produced by muscular contraction is inevitably lost to the exterior when the warmed blood passes through the gills (an effective aquatic respiratory organ is necessarily a competent exchanger of heat, as well as of respiratory gases).

Tunas are unique among teleost fish in being thermoconserving. The vascular anatomy of some species ensures that heat passing from the muscles into the veins is conserved because most of it moves directly from venous to arterial vessels before the venous blood continues to the gills. In the red muscle, parallel arterioles and venules are closely juxtaposed and so ensure that much of the metabolic heat produced during sustained swimming is retained by the musculature. These **counter-current heat exchangers** impose 'thermal barriers' that prevent the dissipation of heat to the surrounding water.

The type and location of such heat exchangers (called **retia mirabilia**, singular **rete mirabile**) vary between the 16 or so species of 'true' tuna, three examples of which are shown in Figure 3.10. In the comparatively primitive skipjack tuna, there is both a well-developed central rete and one pair of small lateral (cutaneous) retia (Figure 3.10a). The most advanced species, such as the three species comprising the bluefin group, and the big-eye tuna, have two pairs of well-developed lateral retia but have completely lost the central rete (Figure 3.10b). The yellowfin tuna is intermediate between these two extremes: it has two pairs of well-developed lateral retia and a small central rete (Figure 3.10c). In the tunas with well-developed lateral retia, the main blood supply to the trunk is through lateral arteries that run along the flank of the fish between the skin and red muscle and give rise to segmental arterioles and venules that form the major blood supply of the white muscles (Figure 3.11). The red muscle on the lateral flank is served by huge numbers of small arteries and veins (about 0.1 mm in diameter) that arise at right angles to the lateral vessels and in some species run along the dorsal and ventral surfaces of the red muscles forming extensive retia mirabilia, consisting of thick bands of arterioles and venules, a few of which give off branches to the muscle (Figure 3.11). In the bluefin tuna, this lateral rete system is the predominant blood supply to both red and white muscle and the dorsal aorta is greatly reduced in size. However, the big-eye tuna, in spite of having well-developed lateral retia, has retained a modest central blood supply.

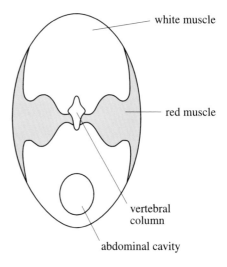

Figure 3.9 An idealized cross-section of the trunk of a tuna, showing the distribution of red and white muscle.

white muscle

red muscle

vertebral column

abdominal cavity

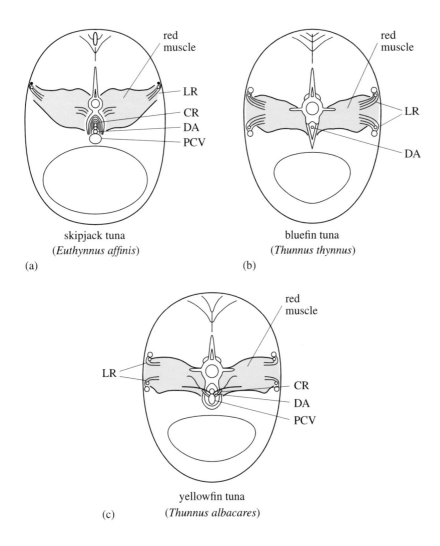

Figure 3.10   Transverse sections of three tuna species showing features related to endothermy. Indicated are the central rete (CR), the lateral retia (LR), the position of red muscle, the dorsal aorta (DA) and the posterior cardinal vein (PCV).

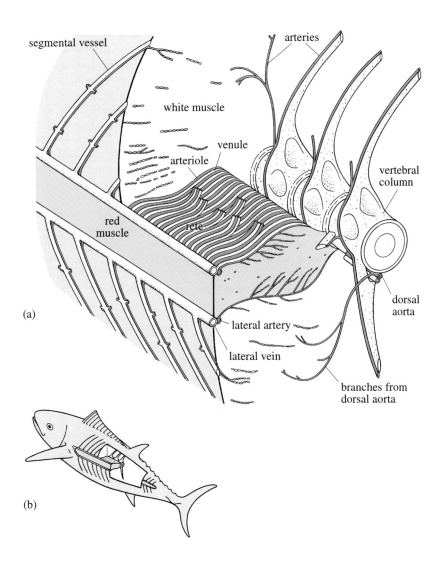

Figure 3.11   An idealized three-dimensional view of the blood circulation in the trunk of a big-eye tuna. The trunk on one side has been cut as shown in diagram (b). The main diagram (a) shows how small arterioles and venules branch from the lateral arteries and veins that run along the surface of the red muscle block, with branches to both white and red tissue. For clarity, the size of the retial vessels is exaggerated. Arterial vessels are shown in blue. Note too the vessels that arise from the dorsal aorta.

As already mentioned, the smaller skipjack tuna have poorly developed lateral retia but a large central rete near the well-developed dorsal aorta. Figures 3.12a and b are schematic drawings of the components of such a central heat exchanger, and Figure 3.12c is a cross-section showing the appearance of the rete and associated tissues *in situ*. Blood that is warmed by muscular metabolism enters the dorsal end of the rete via segmental veins (Figure 3.12a) which eventually break up into numerous thin-walled venules that pass through the rete. Here, this warm blood is close to cool, oxygenated blood within small arterioles that arise from the dorsal aorta. The arterial blood is warmed as it moves through the rete towards the dorsal end, where segmental arterial vessels pass to the musculature (Figure 3.12b). In a 2 kg skipjack, the single central heat exchanger is about 71 mm wide and may contain more than a million exchange vessels, each about 10 mm long. The transfer of heat within the exchanger ensures that warmed venous blood from the muscles is pre-cooled by its passage through the rete before it enters the posterior cardinal vein on the way to the gills; the heat it relinquishes is picked up by the arterial blood flowing out through the segmental arteries. The net effect of the retia is that heat generated during exercise is retained in the muscles. This reduces the extent of heat exchange between the core of the animal and the environment. So, tunas enjoy a substantial **thermal inertia**, which 'dampens' the effect of changes in water temperature. They cool and warm at a rate that is only about 60% of that of typical teleosts of similar weight. Rather more remarkably, skipjack tuna cool and warm less rapidly than many air-breathing reptiles, even though tunas are at a disadvantage because of their aquatic respiration (remember that water not only contains less oxygen per unit volume than air, but also has greater cooling capacity).

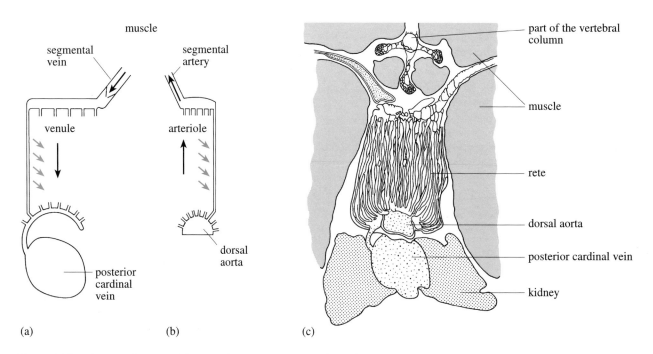

Figure 3.12   The main features of the central vascular heat exchanger of the skipjack tuna. (a) A schematic diagram showing the venous blood supply to and from the rete, represented as a single small venule. (b) The arterial blood flow branching from the dorsal aorta. Blue arrows indicate the movement of heat, and black arrows show blood flow. Note that above the rete, segmental arteries and veins (with valves) convey blood to and from the major muscle mass. (c) Cross-section showing the rete and the associated tissues *in situ*.

A large thermal inertia carries the advantage of a measure of independence from fluctuations in the environmental temperature, which may be greatly advantageous for fish that undertake substantial vertical movements. Some species of marine fish move regularly through the **thermocline,** a layer of water at a depth of 500–1 000 metres, in which there is a fairly rapid temperature transition between the warmer surface waters and the cooler, more dense seawater below. We can calculate that if a tuna swam through the thermocline, it would take 38% longer to cool by 5 °C than would a 'non-tuna'. This would make a great difference to overall performance, which is likely to decrease as core temperature falls. This contrast is strikingly illustrated by recent telemetric data from the wild involving two species of shark: one, the blue shark (*Prionace glauca*) is genuinely poikilothermic and lacks heat exchangers, whereas the other, the mako shark (*Isurus oxyrinchus*), has a high stable visceral temperature by virtue of a large complex rete near the liver. In this instance, the mako shark passed through the thermocline at frequent intervals (Figure 3.13a) but the temperature in the stomach hardly changed during these periods. In contrast, when the blue shark repeatedly swam between the surface and a depth of 250 m, deep-muscle temperature faithfully followed changes in ambient temperature with a brief lag (see Figure 3.13b). In fact, most of the fish that undergo extensive vertical migrations have muscle and visceral temperatures close to ambient water temperatures. The swordfish (*Xiphias gladius*), can be exposed to a change in water temperature of as much as 20°C in less than 2 hours, which is likely to have a major influence on brain function. In fact, the brain and eyes of *Xiphias* and of all tunas examined are always substantially warmer than the surrounding water, although in tunas the excess in the brain and eyes is smaller than that in the muscle. Our knowledge is almost complete for the swordfish, which has a particularly ingenious heater for the brain and eye. A large swelling near the eye muscles, close to the brain case, consists of highly vascularized brown tissue, high in cytochrome c and packed with mitochondria. The blood supply to this tissue is a well-developed rete mirabile, with tightly packed parallel arteries and veins. The temperature within the brown tissue of captured swordfish is about 4 °C above ambient conditions and there is a gradient of temperature along the rete from a value close to that of the environment at the far end, increasing towards the brown tissue.

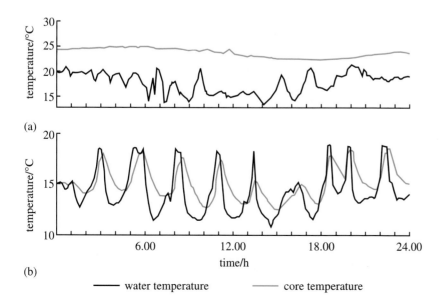

(a)

(b)

water temperature   core temperature

Figure 3.13 Telemetric data showing the core temperatures (blue) and water temperatures (black) for two fish measured over 24 hours in the ocean. (a) In the mako shark (*Isurus oxyrinchus*) core (stomach) temperature remains steady as the fish swims into water of varying temperature. (b) In the blue shark (*Prionace glauca*), which is genuinely poikilothermic, core (deep-muscle) temperature follows changes in the ambient temperature.

■   From this information, what can you deduce about the functions of the brown tissue and the rete?

The present evidence suggests that the brown tissue keeps the eyes and brain relatively warm and functions rather like brown adipose tissues of mammals. The two tissues share many common features, but the thermogenic function of the swordfish brown tissue has yet to be proved conclusively. The rete appears to confine the heat generated by the brown tissue to its immediate vicinity; this property is in contrast to mammalian brown adipose tissue in which the rich blood supply serves to dissipate heat to distant regions.

Is it possible that various types of exchangers in tunas and sharks exchange other things besides heat? If mass transfer (e.g. the transfer of ions and gas) occurred, as well as the transfer of heat, oxygen might pass from the arterioles to the venules in the rete and so threaten oxygen delivery to the tissues. However, if we look at the dimensions of the heat-exchange rete, we see that the arterioles and venules are significantly larger than those in the gills and they are separated by a greater distance, approximately $10 \, \mu m$. Heat diffuses much more rapidly than oxygen, so the dimensions of the heat exchanger are appropriate for the substantial movement of heat and the minimal movement of oxygen.

3.3.2 Thermoregulation in tunas

So far, we have established that tunas conserve metabolic heat and thereby elevate their red-muscle (and possibly white-muscle) temperature. This raises a question of major physiological interest which we can touch on only lightly—do tunas thermoregulate in the mammalian sense, i.e. do they vary the extent of heat production or heat loss and so maintain a relatively constant core temperature, irrespective of fluctuations in ambient temperature?

We can start by looking back at the field data of body temperature of the two species of tuna shown in Figure 3.8. If both species of tuna thermoregulated, their tissue temperature would tend to be constant, and excess temperature would be greater in tunas from cold water than in those from warm water.

■   Does Figure 3.8 provide any such evidence?

In both species body temperature is variable (the scatter of points is appreciable). However, there is little evidence for thermoregulation in the skipjack. In cold waters (20 °C) the excess is similar to that in warm waters. However, in the bluefin, the slope of the regression line relating water and muscle temperature is significantly different from that of the dashed line of a conformer. In water of 7 °C the excess is about 19 °C, but the excess is less than 3 °C in water at 30 °C. So, on this evidence, the bluefin tuna may be a moderately successful thermoregulator. Studies with captive tunas have suggested that they are able to regulate heat transfer to the environment to some extent but this could be through changes in cardiac output (which would affect blood flow rate through the rete), rather than through physiological thermoregulation. Data from field experiments on bluefin tuna and big-eye tuna have been ambiguous and it is only recently that the question of whether tunas perform physiological thermoregulation or not, has been resolved.

■   Can you think of a reason why it would be advantageous for tunas to regulate their heat balance physiologically?

As tunas increase their speed, the amount of heat produced internally rises substantially. As more heat is produced, the activity of the animal increases even more—a type of positive feedback mechanism known in engineering terms as **'thermal runaway'**. This may be an advantage for swimming at high speeds or below the thermocline but it would be counterproductive for a tuna swimming rapidly in warm surface waters. Under these conditions body temperature is likely to rise extremely steeply to injurious levels unless some thermoregulatory mechanism intervenes that permits increased cooling at high levels of activity. One way in which this effect may be minimized is by the evolution of a metabolism that is not dependent on ambient temperature. This remarkable adaptation appears to have evolved in the skipjack tuna—in this species, metabolic rate during normal swimming is constant over a wide range of water temperatures. However, in other tunas, some thermoregulatory ability is a necessity if body temperatures are not to approach lethal limits.

The practical problems of investigating this topic are formidable, but some exciting recent data have emerged from captive tunas held at the Kewalo Research Facility in Honolulu, the only laboratory in the world that maintains live tunas in captivity for research. These results suggest that physiological thermoregulation in tunas is a reality. When rates of heat loss from swimming tunas were estimated at different ambient temperatures, most yellowfin and skipjack tuna showed evidence of increased heat loss at higher water temperatures. When skipjack tuna were forced to swim faster at temperatures close to their lethal limit, the excess temperature fell even though their swimming speed was not reduced. This means that increases in swimming speed (and hence in heat production and cardiac output) are not always accompanied by complementary increases in the excess of body temperature above water temperature. Because excess temperature can change independently of swimming velocity and heat production, it appears that some physiological mechanism regulates the rate of heat dissipation from the body. Tunas are evidently not prisoners of their own heat-conserving mechanisms.

There is in fact new evidence that indicates that the big-eye tuna controls heat dissipation by rerouting arterial blood through the central blood system and thereby effectively disengaging the heat exchangers. In open-ocean tracking experiments Kim Holland and co-workers telemetered swimming depth and body temperature of two big-eye tuna. They found that as the tuna ascended from cold water into warmer surface water or vice versa, the rate of heat transfer with the environment varied rapidly by two orders of magnitude even though metabolic heat production remained constant. To explain these observations, they suggested the following: when the fish ascends after a period of foraging at depth in cold water, the body temperature would be lower than ambient temperature. In order to raise body temperature, the heat exchangers are disengaged and heat transfer with the environment is increased, thereby effectively raising the influx of ambient heat and facilitating the rapid warming of muscle after foraging in cold water. In addition, elevated heat flux with the environment on ascent to warmer waters reduces the risk of overheating. Once the fish descends into deeper colder water, the heat exchangers are reactivated and heat is conserved.

Heidi Dewar and co-workers did a similar study on yellowfin tuna using a water tunnel. In so doing, they were able to rule out the effect of ambient temperature on both metabolic heat production and cardiac output, both of which could affect heat exchange and produce results that mask or mimic physiological thermoregulation. For example, cooler water would reduce heart rate whereas warm water would increase it. Their conclusions to the study were similar to those of Holland and co-workers: that yellowfin tuna are able regulate heat transfer actively (as opposed to passively via changes in metabolic heat output and cardiac output) with changes in ambient temperature. They suggested that the mechanism of regulation is likely to be via changes in blood flow to or through the retia.

■ What are the precise advantages to tunas of their warm bodies?

Some fast-moving fish, e.g. the wahoo (*Acanthocybium solandii*), do not have elevated core temperatures but can swim as fast as tunas. Evidently, high swimming speeds can be achieved in poikilothermic fish, especially in warm water, but sustained cruising at high speed (marathon performances) may depend upon warmth. Tunas are well adapted for high performance during cruising, as evidenced by their ability to swim at speeds of $10\,BL\,s^{-1}$ for much longer periods than most fish of comparable size. As befits high speed cruisers, tunas have relatively more red muscle. Most fish have only about 5% of the muscle bulk as red fibres but, in the skipjack tuna, about 33% of the trunk muscle is composed of internalized red muscle (see Figure 3.9). This arrangement would present a problem for a conventional fish during burst swimming, because at burst speeds the substantial bulk of red muscle contributes little to the power output of the trunk, since, as you know, red fibres contract much more slowly than white ones. In tunas so much of the trunk musculature is red muscle, that it would seriously jeopardise burst performances at very high speeds. These thoughts prompted Ian Johnston and Richard Brill to investigate contraction velocities of red and white muscle fibres from the skipjack tuna to determine, in particular, how the rate of shortening of each fibre changed with temperature. Their results, using single muscle fibres, are shown in Figure 3.14. Suppose the skipjack tuna had a uniform body temperature of 25 °C. At this temperature, the red muscle would contract during burst swimming at a maximum rate of about 3 muscle lengths per second whereas the white muscle would contract at a maximum rate of about 5 muscle lengths per second. However, if, as seems likely, the animal maintained a difference of at least 5 °C in the temperature of red and white muscles, both types of fibre would be able to contract at the same speed (see the black arrow) and hence both could contribute to power production during burst swimming. Indeed, it is noticeable that although both red and white muscles in tunas are warmer than the ambient temperature, red muscle is usually particularly warm. So, although the tuna is specialized for cruising, by keeping its red muscle above ambient temperature, it may avoid compromising performance at very high speeds.

This idea is exciting, but is only one of several theories that seek to explain how an elevation of muscle temperature promotes fast, sustained swimming. An alternative suggestion is that the warmth of tuna muscle permits a very high rate of oxygen delivery. Tuna muscle may take up oxygen at a high rate (and display a high aerobic capacity) because of the large amount of red muscle myoglobin.

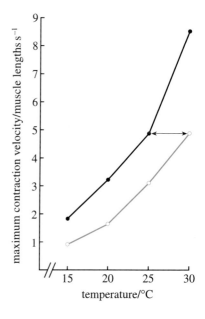

Figure 3.14   The effect of temperature on the contraction velocity of internally located deep slow red muscle fibres (blue line) and fast white muscle fibres (black line). A temperature difference of approximately 51°C has been reported for skipjack tuna, in which case the contraction speeds for red and white muscle fibres are the same (see the black arrow).

■ Can you think of another likely function of myoglobin?

Rather than acting just as an oxygen store, myoglobin also facilitates the delivery of oxygen to the mitochondria.

Elevated tissue temperature has only a very small effect on the diffusion of free oxygen, but it has a very pronounced effect on the myoglobin-aided flux of oxygen to the mitochondria. The facilitated diffusion of oxygen may increase by about 40% if muscle temperature is raised by 10 °C. This increased delivery of oxygen to the mitochondria would enable tunas to maintain high rates of aerobic metabolism and may well represent one major advantage of body warmth.

Summary of Section 3.3

Tunas (and some sharks) have counter-current heat exchangers (called retia mirabilia) which conserve metabolic heat and maintain the locomotor muscles at elevated temperatures. Retia are associated with the viscera and with the eyes and brain, but muscle temperatures in tuna are raised primarily by lateral retia (as in the bluefin tuna) or by a large central exchanger (as in the skipjack tuna). In both types, venous and arterial vessels are in close proximity and heat that would otherwise be lost via the gills diffuses from the warm venous blood into the cooler arterial blood flowing in the opposite direction. This conservation of heat gives most tunas a large thermal inertia, which means that they are to some degree shielded from the effects of fluctuations in environmental temperature. Elevated tissue temperatures may offer several advantages that enable tunas to sustain high-speed cruising for prolonged periods. At high swimming speeds, a temperature difference between internalized red and white muscle may enable both types of muscle fibres to contract at a similar velocity and therefore contribute to power production. Another possibility is that raised muscle temperatures increase the rate at which myoglobin delivers oxygen to the muscle mitochondria. Indeed, tunas do display extremely high rates of oxygen uptake and their muscles are rich in myoglobin. There is now substantial evidence to suggest that tunas can thermoregulate. However, the exact physiological mechanisms employed remain to be elucidated.

3.4 Conclusion

Muscular tissue forms a larger part of the mass of the fish body than it does of other vertebrates. Approximately 40–60% of the total body mass of most fish is locomotor muscle. This is partly because economy in weight is not mandatory, as it is for terrestrial animals and birds, and partly because of the demands placed on the locomotor system by the density of the water—a large amount of muscle is required to generate sufficient power for rapid swimming. In fish, muscle fibres are divided into slow, red fibres and fast, white fibres. Red muscle fibres are used mainly for sustained, steady swimming and metabolic energy is derived mainly from aerobic metabolism. White muscle fibres, on the other hand, function as an 'emergency power pack' and in most fish are active only during brief, intense bouts of burst swimming. The function of white muscle fibres in powering fast bursts of swimming is facilitated partly by their complex helical arrangement. This arrangement allows them to contract over a shorter distance than the red fibres, given the same body curvature. The shorter distance decreases the contraction velocity during the fast movements which they power, and brings it into the range where they can generate maximum power.

Elevated tissue temperatures have enabled tunas to approach what has been termed the 'ragged edge of piscine existence', where they have very nearly overcome some of the design problems inherent in the fish body plan. Their elevated muscle temperature has enabled them to attain rates of metabolism close to that of mammals, and levels of activity greater than those of any other teleost. They have properly been termed 'energy speculators'—these fast-swimming fish gamble a large expenditure (i.e. high activity) on the expectation of similarly large energy returns as food. They form an extreme contrast to other large fish, 'the energy frugalists', which survive by cutting energy expenditure to a minimum and adopting a near-planktonic existence (e.g. the ocean sunfish).

Objectives for Chapter 3

After completing Chapter 3 you should be able to:

3.1   Define and use, or recognize definitions and applications of, each of the **bold** terms.

3.2   Identify the structural, biochemical, physiological and functional characteristics of red and white muscle.

3.3   Explain how power is transferred from the anterior myotomes to the caudal fin during swimming.

3.4   Draw diagrams to explain how the central and lateral heat exchangers of tunas conserve heat, and suggest two likely advantages to tuna of elevated muscle temperatures.

3.5   Outline and interpret experiments that would test the ability of tunas to thermoregulate.

Questions for Chapter 3

(Answers to questions are at the end of the book.)

Question 3.1 (Objective 3.2)

Which of the following descriptions (a–f) relate to white (fast) fibres of fish, and which relate to red (slow) fibres? Gve reasons for your answers. To answer some of the questions you will need to make *deductions* from the information given in Section 3.2.

(a)   The fibres have a relatively large diameter and can be either focally or multiply innervated.

(b)   The myofibrils are very densely packed and there are fewer mitochondria.

(c)   In all fish, these fibres receive a similar type of innervation and contain significant amounts of stored lipid.

(d)   The enzymes citrate synthetase and cytochrome oxidase have greater activities in these muscle fibres.

(e)   In the trout, aerobic metabolism in these fibres is greater than that in the corresponding tissue of other 'primitive' teleosts; for example, it has significant cytochrome oxidase activity.

(f)   In the dogfish, lactate is likely to accumulate in these fibres during burst swimming.

Question 3.2 (Objective 3.2)

The mass of red fibres in the myotomes of three different teleosts has been measured and expressed as a percentage of the total trunk musculature. The measured values were species A, 29.8%; species B, 72.8%; species C, 5.5%. One fish (mackerel) is an active swimmer, swimming constantly at high speeds; the second (the angler fish) is a sedentary bottom-dweller and the third is an active swimmer, but swims at sustained speeds mainly using enlarged pectoral fins. From your knowledge of the function of red muscle, identify A, B and C.

Question 3.3 (Objective 3.2)

(a)   In mammalian muscle, glycogen breakdown is initiated by means of blood-borne hormones which activate phosphorylase enzymes (via a number of intermediate steps). However, no such mechanism operates in the white muscle of dogfish. Instead, phosphorylase is activated directly by calcium released from the sarcoplasmic reticulum. Can you suggest one reason why the mammalian type of activation might be inappropriate in dogfish white muscle?

(b)   Proteins called parvalbumins are found in high concentrations in fish white muscle fibres. Their most likely role is that they allow rapid relaxation of the muscle. Why might these proteins be particularly important in the white muscle of relatively small fish during burst swimming?

Question 3.4 (Objective 3.2)

Which of the following statements (a–f) is the most accurate?

(a)   All of the accumulated lactate produced from burst swimming is exported to the fish liver where it acts as a gluconeogenic substrate.

(b)   The oxidation of lactate by fish muscle requires the utilization of oxygen, whereas the conversion of lactate into glucose does not require oxygen directly or indirectly.

(c)   A gluconeogenic role for red muscle is clearly indicated by it having high activities of the key enzymes involved, for example PEP carboxykinase.

(d)   During burst swimming, lactic acid is immediately released from white muscle and circulates in the blood where it may produce a change in pH that could influence the carrying capacity of the pigment.

(e)   Most of the accumulated lactate produced from burst swimming is oxidized during recovery. However some lactate may be converted into glucose within the white muscle, given that, in some species, white muscle has an appreciable aerobic potential.

(f)   The duration of burst swimming is probably limited by the level of accumulated lactate in exercising muscles, although it might be extended by the rapid export of lactate to the red muscle.

Question 3.5 (Objectives 3.2 and 3.3)

(a)   Why do fish myotomes contain a range of muscle fibre types?

(b)   Which muscle fibre type has the highest gearing ratio and what are the advantages of this arrangement?

(c)   What is the consequence of the wave of body curvature and the activation of lateral muscles travelling at different rates along the body of a fish?

Question 3.6 (Objective 3.4)

Classify each of the following statements (a–g) as true or false and explain why.

(a)   Tunas are unique amongst fish in that they possess heat exchangers that elevate muscle and visceral temperatures.

(b)   In the skipjack tuna, pre-cooled blood within the posterior cardinal vein passes toward the heart and into the gills.

(c)   Tunas can properly be termed endotherms, although the inability of the skipjack tuna to thermoregulate means that this species is a true poikilotherm.

(d)   Because white muscle in tuna is exclusively an anaerobic tissue, it cannot be a site for the production and conservation of metabolic heat.

(e)   Because tunas possess heat exchangers, they may be able to make excursions into the cold water beneath the thermocline without a sharp drop in body temperature.

(f)   One advantage that tunas may gain from being warm is that an increase in tissue temperature greatly enhances the rate of oxygen supply to the mitochondria by simple diffusion.

(g)   Only fish that have elevated muscle temperatures can swim relatively fast.

A known quantity of heat was applied to the gills of skipjack tuna. This heat pulse was transferred to the blood passing through the gills and appeared in the dorsal aorta. It was noted that: (i) muscle temperature was unaffected by the heat pulse; (ii) a significant proportion (about 80%) of the added heat appeared in the blood sampled from the ventral aorta (which carries deoxygenated blood from the heart to the gills). What does this result tell you about the effectiveness of the central heat exchanger?

Which, if any, of the following observations and experiments (a–g) provide evidence that tunas are able to regulate their body temperature?

(a) Most of the heat generated by red muscle during swimming in tunas is prevented from leaving the muscle by central or lateral heat exchangers.

(b) When ambient temperature is decreased, tunas show no increase in metabolic rate.

(c) During routine swimming, skipjack tuna maintain a constant metabolic rate over a wide range of ambient temperatures.

(d) When bluefin tuna swim into water of very different temperature, their body temperature changes only very little or very slowly.

(e) Excess temperatures in wild bluefin tuna are greater in animals caught in cold waters than those recorded from warm waters.

(f) Skipjack tuna appear to reduce the intensity and duration of their bouts of activity when their body temperature approaches a critically high value of about 35 °C.

(g) If skipjack tuna are encouraged to increase their swimming speed dramatically, there is no appreciable increase in their excess temperature.

CHAPTER 4 BUOYANCY AND DEPTH

Prepared for the Course Team by Mandy Dyson

4.1 Introduction

When a fish is totally immersed in water it displaces an amount of water equal to its body volume. If the weight of the displaced water is greater than the weight of the fish, the fish is said to be positively buoyant and will tend to float. If the weight of the water is less than that of the fish, the fish is said to be be negatively buoyant and will tend to sink. If the weight of the displaced water equals that of the fish, the fish is said to be neutrally buoyant. So, underwater, the weight of an animal is counteracted by its buoyancy. This is the basis of Archimedes' principle, which states that a body immersed in a fluid experiences an upthrust or buoyancy equal to the weight of the displaced mass of the fluid (water in this case).

Buoyancy is given by :

$$A \text{ (buoyancy)} = V\rho_w g$$

where V is the volume of the animal, ρ_w is the density of water and g is the acceleration due to gravity (a constant).

The weight of the animal is given by:

$$W \text{ (weight)} = V\rho_a g$$

where ρ_a is the average density of the animal.

So, an animal that is neutrally buoyant has a density (ρ_a) equal to the density of the water in which it is submerged (ρ_w). Under this condition, the upward force of buoyancy (A) will exactly balance the downward force of weight (W).

So if a fish or any other aquatic animal were made of materials that were of the same density (density = mass/volume) as the water in which it lived, it would not weigh anything in water, and would be neutrally buoyant (Chapter 1). Seawater has a density of around 1.03 g cm^{-3} and freshwater one of around 1.00 g cm^{-3} (at 1 atmosphere and 15 °C) but most animal tissues are of greater density. Muscles are full of contractile proteins with densities around 1.33 g cm^{-3}, and skeletal tissues such as bone may be so loaded with calcium salts that their density is over 2.00 g cm^{-3} There are, of course, some less dense substances in most animals, such as fats of different kinds, and many marine animals (including bony fish) have body fluids that are more dilute than seawater (and are hence less dense). In general, one can assume that the densities of marine animals are around 1.06– 1.09 g cm^{-3}, i.e. they are some 5% denser than seawater and so tend to sink. In other words, these animals are negatively buoyant. For example, a mackerel that weighs 500 g in air weighs around 25 g in seawater, and in effect climbs a 1 in 15 hill all its life just to stay at the same depth in the sea and not sink. You can check this assumption yourself by weighing a fresh fish, e.g. a mackerel, in air, and then weighing it in water by suspending it from a small spring balance or bathroom scales. You can do this by putting a rod or a coat hanger across the scales and tying cotton to each end so that you can hang the fish from it (Figure 4.1). If you have weighed the fish in seawater you will find that the 5% difference in weight is about right, but if you do not live by the sea and so use freshwater, you will find the fish weighs about 7% of its weight in air.

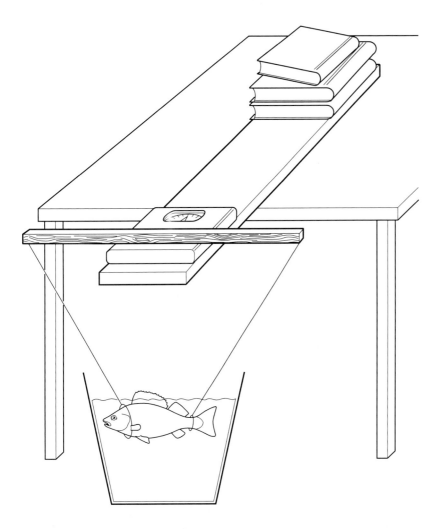

Figure 4.1   How to weigh a fish in water with bathroom scales.

Many scombrid fish (tuna, bonito, mackerel) have an average density greater than that of seawater. This means that the upward acting buoyancy force is not great enough to completely cancel the downward acting force of weight so that without an additional upward force, they would sink. One method of balancing these upward and downward forces is through the use of **hydrodynamic lift** (Section 2.3.3). Hydrodynamic lift is generated by the extended pectoral fins and, to a lesser extent, by the tail as the fish swims forward. Lift from the pectorals needs to be much greater than that from the tail because in most fish, the centre of buoyancy (determined by the distribution of volume along the body), and the centre of mass (determined by the relative densities of the different parts of the body), are usually nearer to the head than the tail due to the dense skull and jaws (Figure 4.2). In fish such as scombrids, which swim with the body horizontal, the two centres are always either in the same place, or just above each other. Lift from the tail therefore acts much further from the centre of buoyancy than does lift from the pectorals, and hence need not be so great.

We might suppose that because shark skeletons are cartilaginous, and cartilage is less dense than bone, sharks without buoyancy mechanisms that lower their density would be less dense and weigh less in water than similarly sized bony fish without buoyancy mechanisms. However, shark cartilage is strengthened by calcifications, and there are very dense denticles (tooth-like structures) in the skin. Shark skeletons are also more solidly built than the strutted girder-like bones of bony fish and, like most bony fish, weigh in seawater about 5% of their weight in air. Almost all sharks balance their weight in water by generating hydrodynamic lift with their outspread pectoral fins, and they also generate lift by setting their caudal fin at a slight angle as it sweeps from side to side (Section 2.3.3). The asymmetrical tail fins of sharks (where the upper lobe is supported by the upturned end of the vertebral column—the **heterocercal** condition) may have evolved because sharks are denser than seawater, and gain lift from the angle taken up by the more flexible lower lobe. However, there are sharks that are neutrally buoyant, and these too have heterocercal tails (Figure 4.3). In fact, in all sharks the angle of the lower lobe can be adjusted to give either lift or downthrust.

The density of air is so much lower than that of the materials from which animals are made that no flying animal can have the same density as air (as balloons and airships do). However, water is sufficiently dense for it to be possible for animals to store enough light substances to achieve neutral buoyancy. Neutral buoyancy is an advantage because it enables fish to save energy in two ways, and furthermore, to behave in ways that negatively buoyant fish cannot:

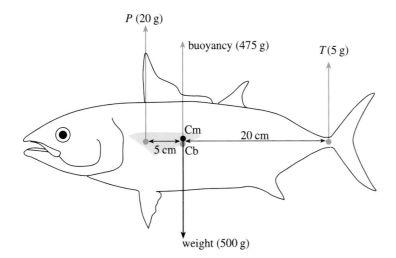

Figure 4.2   In this fish the centre of buoyancy (Cb) is situated just below the centre of mass (Cm). Because the density of the fish is greater than that of water, the weight is greater than buoyancy. Lift is generated by the tail (T) and the pectorals (P). Since lift generated by the tail acts further from the centre of buoyancy than does lift generated by the pectorals, it need not be as great.

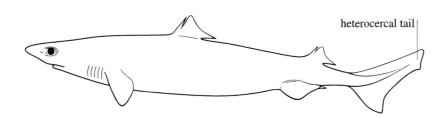

Figure 4.3   The neutrally buoyant deep-sea squaloid shark (*Centroscymnus*). Note that it has small pectoral fins that do not generate significant lift in level swimming.

1   Only neutrally buoyant fish can hover practically motionless in water. This ability is a great advantage for not only can such fish remain in position without expending muscular effort, but they can also hover or swim very slowly whilst seeking their prey. The John Dory (*Zeus faber*; Figure 2.13f), for example, is almost perfectly neutrally buoyant and sidles slowly to within range of unsuspecting small fish and crustaceans, whereupon it engulfs them by shooting out its protractile jaws. Similarly, deep sea angler fish hang in ambush in the water waiting for their prey to come within reach of their jaws. Marine fish without buoyancy organs have to generate an upward lift force (equivalent to 5% of their body weight) to stay at one level; to do this they have to move forwards all the time, and cannot remain stationary to lurk for their prey.

2   Neutral buoyancy saves a substantial proportion of the energy costs of forward movement. When a negatively buoyant fish swims at about 3–4 bodylengths per second, as much as 20% of the total power for movement is committed to overcoming the tendency to sink. As a result, a fish without a buoyancy mechanism needs a greater power output (and therefore an increased energy outlay, and a higher rate of oxygen consumption) to swim horizontally at a given speed, than does a neutrally buoyant fish.

These advantages appear so significant that it is at first sight rather surprising that there are many active fish which are *not* neutrally buoyant. As already mentioned, most scombrid fish are negatively buoyant. There are even some fish which seem to regulate their density carefully, not to that for neutral buoyancy, but to some density intermediate between that for neutral buoyancy and that for fish without any buoyancy mechanisms! We can easily imagine that for sluggish fish that spend most of their time resting on the bottom, such as dogfish or plaice, it would not be worth achieving neutral buoyancy, and in fact such fish are not neutrally buoyant. But why are many active fish, such as mackerel, not neutrally buoyant? To understand why, we need to examine the materials that provide fish with a source of **static lift**, namely lipids and gas.

4.2 Lipids as a source of static lift

Lipids have virtually the same compressibility as water, so the static lift provided by lipids in a fish remains almost the same when the ambient pressure alters as the fish changes depth. This gives lipids a great advantage over gas in providing static lift, because the lift given by gas varies with ambient pressure unless it is stored in a strong rigid container. Indeed, many of the small myctophids (lantern fish), which make extensive daily vertical migrations to and from the surface of the sea, begin life by storing gas in a non-rigid, soft-walled container, the swimbladder, but as they grow older, gradually replace the gas with lipid. Ordinary fish lipids, such as cod liver oil, have densities of around $0.93 \, \text{g cm}^{-3}$, but lipids used to give enough lift for neutral buoyancy are special lipids of lower density. Deep-sea sharks, basking sharks and a few teleosts store the hydrocarbon squalene, whilst many myctophids, together with the coelacanth (*Latimeria chalumnae*) and the castor-oil fish (*Ruvettus pretiosus*), store wax esters. Both of these special low-density kinds of lipid have densities of around $0.86 \, \text{g cm}^{-3}$.

■   Can you think of a disadvantage of using lipids to provide static lift?

Unlike gas, lipids such as squalene and wax esters have a density which is not greatly different to that of seawater, so neutral buoyancy is attainable only if relatively large deposits are accumulated. The metabolic cost of synthesizing these stores is substantial and more must be added as the animal grows. Lipid synthesis is not rapid enough to take account of short-term density increases such as occur after swallowing a large dense meal. However, many of the deep-sea sharks, e.g. the squaloid shark (*Centroscymnus*; Figure 4.3) attain neutral buoyancy because their enormous livers, which occupy 30% of the volume of the body, contain so much squalene (about 80%) that they provide just enough lift to compensate exactly for the weight in water of the denser parts of the body. Some of these neutrally buoyant deep-sea sharks store so much lipid (and are corpulent as a result) without reducing the dense components of their bodies that, if the liver is removed, they weigh in seawater just under 5% of their weight (less the liver) in air. Others, such as the bramble shark (*Echinorhinus*) have poorly calcified vertebrae and thin skins, and without their livers weigh in water only around 2% of their weight in air; hence they need to store relatively less lipid.

The large basking shark (*Cetorhinus*), which cruises slowly along with its mouth open, sieving plankton, also depends upon squalene in its huge liver to achieve near-neutral buoyancy, and a basking shark weighing nearly 2 000 kg in air (measured with a 5-ton crane!) was found to weigh less than 2 kg in water. Basking sharks swim at around 1 m s^{-1} when feeding, which seems to be a good speed for filter feeding—the other huge elasmobranch filter feeders, the devil fish (*Mobula*) and the whale shark (*Rhincodon*), also swim at this speed. Basking sharks have to be close to neutral buoyancy because they cannot generate sufficient hydrodynamic lift at this slow swimming speed. The deep-sea squaloid sharks and the basking shark store sufficient lipid to attain neutral buoyancy, but the great majority of sharks do not. Bottom-living sharks such as the dogfish (*Scyliorhinus*) are inactive by day, resting on the sea bottom, and it is not necessary for them to achieve neutral buoyancy. However, most fast-swimming sharks like the spurdog (*Squalus acanthias*), or the blue shark (*Prionace glauca*) store lipid to reduce their density, but not in sufficient quantity to be neutrally buoyant. Some reduction in density is advantageous, because they can reduce the size of the pectoral fins used to generate lift (and so reduce the energy expended during swimming by reducing drag), but there is a limit to this reduction since the fins are used for manoeuvring and, unlike the fins of bony fish, cannot be furled.

Many of the fish living in the depths of the sea avoid the difficulties of lipid storage by greatly reducing their dense components, so that they need little lipid to achieve neutral or near-neutral buoyancy. They have watery muscles, there are often large subcutaneous sinuses and pockets containing a lymph less dense than seawater, and in the skeleton only the jaws are well calcified. Such fish have an extremely high water content: the angler fish (*Melanocetus*) is 95% water, the gulper eel (*Eurypharynx*) 94% and the bristlemouth (*Gonostoma*) 90%. In contrast, fish that use gas for static lift (see Section 4.3.1) can afford to support the dense components of their bodies without difficulty, and the lantern fish and the curiously flattened hatchet fish are much less watery and have fully calcified skeletons. The buoyancy balance sheets in Figure 4.4 show the differences between the bristlemouth (*Gonostoma*), a fish that stores lipid and hence has greatly reduced dense components, and a shallow-water wrasse (*Ctenolabrus*), which uses gas for static lift and hence can afford to support much more dense body components.

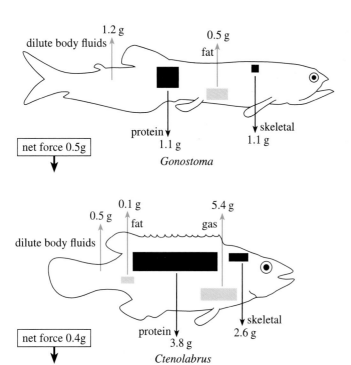

Figure 4.4   The buoyancy balance sheets of the watery fish *Gonostoma*, which lacks a swimbladder, and the shallow-water wrasse *Ctenolabrus*, which has a gas-filled swimbladder. The figures given are per 100 g of fish. Notice the differences in the weight of the dense body components. The net balance of the forces identified for each fish is shown on the left.

Summary of Section 4.2

Fish composed of materials that are more dense than seawater weigh more than the volume of water they displace, i.e. they are negatively buoyant. Such fish can avoid sinking when swimming by generating hydrodynamic lift, mainly by using their outstretched pectoral fins as hydrofoils. For fish that normally rest on the sea bottom, negative buoyancy may be an advantage, but when fish are free-swimming, generating lift hydrodynamically represents a substantial drain on the resources for locomotion because it demands an increased expenditure of energy. Except for very fast-moving fish, a better solution is to acquire static lift and become weightless in water by accumulating light materials, particularly lipid and gas but also, in the deep sea, dilute body fluids. Lipid has the advantage that it is virtually incompressible and offers a constant amount of lift irrespective of depth, but it is also inconveniently bulky, because relatively large amounts are required.

4.3 Gas as a source of static lift

Animals that use gas for buoyancy face a quite different set of problems, and some of the most remarkable adaptations in the whole animal kingdom have resulted from the need to overcome them. If the animal is 'designed' to float at the surface, then gas is an excellent source of lift, for little is required and, moreover, it is not difficult to confine or secrete gas against atmospheric pressure. Several of the remarkable planktonic siphonophores (a specialized group within the phylum Cnidaria, including the Portuguese man-of-war, *Physalia)* float in this way at the surface. Most aquatic animals, however, do not use gas for floating, but to achieve neutral buoyancy; these animals are subject to changes in ambient pressure when they move to different depths. For every

10 metres of increased depth in the sea, hydrostatic pressure increases by 101.3 kPa. So any animal that uses gas in this way faces considerable problems. In some animals, the gas is confined within a rigid box, so that when they change depth the volume of the box always remains the same (and hence the lift generated by the contained gas does not vary). This solution is adopted by the cephalopod molluscs (especially the cuttlefish *Sepia* and *Nautilus*) and was probably used by the abundant fossil ammonites. It works well within certain depth limits but, just like deep-sea diving suits, the box containing gas has to be very strongly constructed to withstand the ambient pressure. Cuttlefish, for example, cannot go below 200 m without their buoyancy organ, the cuttlebone, imploding. As we might guess, they live in shallower water! Here we concentrate on fish where the gas is held in a non-rigid soft-walled container, the swimbladder.

4.3.1 Buoyancy from elastic gas-filled swimbladders

Most (but not all) teleosts have elastic gas-filled swimbladders that are approximately oval and located above the abdominal cavity beneath the vertebral column (Figure 4.5).

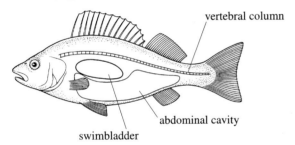

vertebral column

abdominal cavity

swimbladder

Figure 4.5 The location of the swimbladder in a 'typical' teleost showing its relationship to the vertebral column and abdominal cavity. Because the swimbladder lies below the dense backbone, the centre of buoyancy is usually just below the centre of mass, which is why fish turn belly up when they die.

Because gases have low densities, only quite small amounts of gas are necessary to match the density of the fish to the surrounding water. Suppose that a fish without a swimbladder has an overall density of 1.07 g cm^{-3}. If the fish weighs 107g in air it displaces 100 cm^3 of water. Knowing the relative densities of seawater (1.03 g cm^{-3}) and freshwater (1.00 g cm^{-3}), we can calculate that the fish weighs 4.0 g in seawater (107−103) and 7.0 g (107−100) in freshwater. If the volume of the fish is increased by only 4.0 cm^3 in seawater or 7.0 cm^3 in freshwater by a swimbladder filled with 'weightless' gas, the fish is neutrally buoyant. By accumulating gas, the fish is increasing its volume without changing its mass and so its overall density is reduced. In fact, although the shape of swimbladders varies a good deal (partly because they may be involved in functions like sound production and hearing as well as in buoyancy), their volume in marine fish is usually about 5% of the total body volume. In freshwater species the swimbladder (as we would expect) is larger, usually some 7% of the body volume. However, there are some freshwater fish, such as the primitive garpike (*Lepisosteus*) of the Americas, which are covered with thick heavy scales and their swimbladders are as much as 12% of their total body volume.

Although fish using gas for neutral buoyancy need to store relatively little gas compared with the sharks and other fish which have to store large amounts of lipid, gas storage involves some serious difficulties.

Swimbladders are compliant and elastic, and not rigid boxes like the buoyancy organs of cephalopods, so if the ambient pressure changes when the fish swims up and down in the water, the swimbladder changes its volume. In general, when fish are subject to transient small-scale changes in pressure, the swimbladder gas obeys Boyle's law* reasonably well (Figure 4.6).

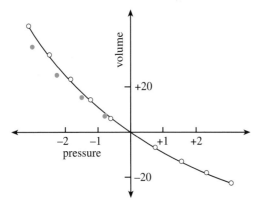

Figure 4.6   Volume changes of an air bubble (open circles) and a freshwater fish swimbladder (blue circles) as ambient pressure changes, showing that for small changes in ambient pressure, the swimbladder gas nearly obeys Boyle's law.

It is easy to see that obeying Boyle's law produces a major problem for fish using gas to achieve neutral buoyancy, unless they swim only at one depth. Suppose that a fish swimbladder is filled with a fixed mass of gas and that the fish is neutrally buoyant.

■   What happens when it changes depth?

If it swims deeper, where the surrounding hydrostatic pressure is greater, the pressure change is transmitted through the body, the swimbladder is compressed and the overall density of the fish increases. The fish will tend to sink further and unless it wants to continue to go deeper, has to generate hydrodynamic lift by swimming actively to remain at this new greater depth. This requirement is not too serious because, even if the swimbladder were to be fully compressed, the difference in density between the fish and water is relatively slight, and in any case the fish is no worse off than other fish which do not have swimbladders! But suppose that the fish swims upwards, perhaps in pursuit of prey, or to escape from a predator. The fish is now in a much more risky situation. Because the external pressure decreases, the swimbladder expands and so the density of the fish decreases. This increased buoyancy sweeps the fish nearer the surface, increasing the swimbladder volume even more and making the fish even more buoyant. Although for small positive changes in buoyancy the fish could actively swim downwards, this process of positive feedback may increase the buoyancy of the fish to such a degree that it cannot swim downwards hard enough and so rises helplessly to the surface. Experiments with cod have shown that they can cope with reductions of 25% below the pressure to which they were originally adapted. When fish are brought up on deep-sea long lines, their swimbladders have expanded to such an extent that when they are brought to the surface they float. In fact, their swimbladders have often burst. Fish are of course not designed to be fished at depth, and then brought rapidly to the surface!

*At a constant temperature, the volume (V) of a given mass of gas is inversely proportional to the pressure (P). The product PV is therefore constant.

So fish with swimbladders suffer from **vertical instability**, because any movement away from buoyancy equilibrium at one depth produces accelerated upward or downward displacement.

■   How might fish maintain neutral buoyancy during variations in ambient pressure caused by changes in depth?

The obvious solution is to maintain a constant gas volume despite changes in depth. Remember that density is mass/volume, which means that fish have to change the mass of the gas within the swimbladder. This conclusion may be obvious, but it is not a simple matter, for fish need mechanisms for inflating and deflating the swimbladder in a controlled way, and at the same time the swimbladder has to be impermeable or the gas would soon diffuse out of it. To remain neutrally buoyant, fish have to decrease the mass of gas within the swimbladder as they ascend in the water and increase it as they descend. Such adjustments present formidable difficulties and fish such as cod or swordfish, which undertake large vertical movements, cannot maintain neutral buoyancy throughout their depth range and, indeed, may be neutrally buoyant only at the top of this range. What is more, because the swimbladder is elastic, the total pressure of the gases inside is normally identical to the ambient hydrostatic pressure, and yet there are fish which manage to use gas-filled swimbladders even at the greatest depths of the oceans. As we shall see, the ways in which fish have solved the problems inherent in using elastic gas containers may justly be regarded as being among the greatest feats of biological engineering. Most of our knowledge comes from studies of shallow-water marine species, but the swimbladders of freshwater fish, and of deep-sea fish (where the problems are most acute) are of essentially the same design, and are likely to function in much the same way.

In general, fish living near the surface have swimbladder gas that resembles air in composition (i.e. about 80% nitrogen, and 20% oxygen), but the proportion of oxygen in the swimbladder is greater in species from greater depths (Figure 4.7).

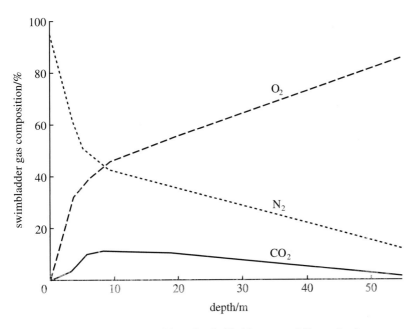

Figure 4.7   Percentage composition of swimbladder gas at different depths.

This fact was discovered in dramatic style in 1803 by the French physicist, Jean-Baptiste Biot, whose primary interest was the composition of the atmosphere. He placed samples of air in a delicate glass gas analyser, added excess hydrogen and sparked the mixture. By weighing the resultant water, the oxygen content of the sample could be established. Perhaps bored by the constancy of atmospheric oxygen, he introduced a sample of swimbladder gas from a deep-sea fish—the resulting explosion wrecked his apparatus! Realizing that this observation meant that the swimbladder gas contained more oxygen than did air, he was able to show, using a new gas analyser, that the proportion of oxygen in swimbladders increased with depth and that the swimbladders of deep-sea fish contained almost pure oxygen. In contrast, it was later found that the gas in the swimbladder is almost entirely nitrogen in some freshwater salmonids (*Coregonus*).

Neutral buoyancy can be achieved at different depths by varying the amount of gas in the swimbladder in such a way that the gas volume is held constant, regardless of external hydrostatic pressure. Fish therefore face two problems: decreasing the mass of gas within the swimbladder as they ascend in water and increasing the mass of contained gas as they descend. Such adjustments present formidable difficulties: because the swimbladder is elastic, the total pressure of gas inside is normally identical to ambient hydrostatic pressure. To see how formidable a task the fish faces with a gas-filled swimbladder when the ambient pressure is high, think of the oxygen-filled swimbladder of deep-sea fish that live at $4\,000$ m below sea level (some may live at $7\,000$ m—a depth of over 4 miles!). Remember that for every 10 m of increased depth in the sea, hydrostatic pressure increases by 101.3 kPa. At a depth of $4\,000$ m, the external pressure will therefore be about 400×10^2 kPa and the total gas pressure within the swimbladder must be the same. The partial pressure of oxygen (P_{O_2}) in the swimbladder is also about 400×10^2 kPa; if 5% of the gas was nitrogen, the partial pressure of nitrogen (P_{N_2}) would be about 20×10^2 kPa and the P_{O_2} would be 380×10^2 kPa. The P_{O_2} and P_{N_2} in the ambient water at this depth would be no greater than about 20 and 80 kPa, respectively, and the partial pressures of these gases in the blood would be about the same. On descent, and even at constant depth (because there may be some slow loss of gas from the swimbladder), fish therefore may have to add oxygen to the swimbladder *against* the huge partial pressure gradient of no less than 2 000:1 ($400 \times 10^2 : 20$ kPa)! Remarkably, this inward movement of oxygen does not occur by active transport of oxygen but by free diffusion of the gas, although the process is somewhat misleadingly called **oxygen secretion**.

A third major difficulty faced by such deep-water teleosts is that the swimbladder wall must be impermeable to prevent the contained gas at high partial pressures from diffusing out into the surrounding tissues.

4.3.2 Structure of the swimbladder

In development, the teleost swimbladder forms as a pouch from the roof of the foregut, and in some more primitive bony fish such as herring, eels and salmonids, the connection between the oesophagus and the swimbladder remains as an open pneumatic duct in the adult (Figure 4.8a). In the majority of teleosts with swimbladders, however, this connection is lost during development, and the adult swimbladder is a closed sac (Figure 4.8b). It is not known why the open duct to the oesophagus has been abandoned in the great majority of the advanced teleosts. There are a number of obvious advantages for shallow-water fish in having an open duct—for example, the swimbladder can easily be emptied, and filled again at the surface by gulping air. As herring ascend in the water towards the surface, they release gas from the anus and so keep swimbladder volume (and hence their density) the same. Fish such as cod, have closed swimbladders and cannot swim near to the surface. Presumably there are greater advantages in sealing off the swimbladder since the great majority of fish have this arrangement, but we have no idea what these may be!

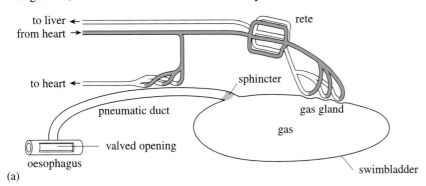

(a)

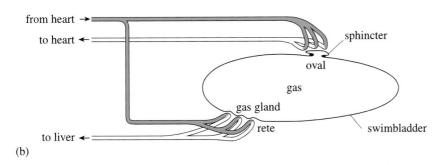

(b)

Figure 4.8 (a) An open swimbladder, as in the eel (*Anguilla anguilla*). Note that the herring, which also has an open swimbladder, lacks the gas gland and the pneumatic duct opens into the stomach, so the swimbladder of the eel should not be thought of as a 'typical' open swimbladder. (b) A swimbladder of the closed type as, for example, in the perch (*Perca fluviatilis*). Arterial vessels in both (a) and (b) are shown in blue.

In both types (though not in herring, which can only fill their swimbladders by gulping air at the surface) there is a special region, the **gas gland**, where gas is 'secreted'. We know this is the site of secretion because when actively secreting swimbladders are cut open, the gas gland is covered with foamy mucus. The foam contains bubbles of oxygen, and experiments with oxygen isotopes have shown that molecular gas moves into the swimbladder from the blood. The blood supply to the gas gland is peculiar in that the incoming capillaries form an elaborate network with the outgoing capillaries that lie close to them. This rete mirabile (seen in Figure 4.8, and in more detail in Figure 4.9a) consists of a staggeringly large number of capillaries running parallel to each other. In the eel, it has been estimated that there are no fewer than 116 000 arterial capillaries closely apposed to 88 000 venous capillaries! The precise relationship between the rete and the gas gland (where the blind-ending loops of the capillaries lie) varies, but the essential point is that arterial blood moving towards the swimbladder and returning venous blood are in intimate contact (see the cross-section of the rete, Figure 4.9b), forming a **counter-current exchanger**. A similar counter-current exchanger (used for a different purpose) is found in the muscles of warm-bodied tuna and sharks (see Section 3.3.1). The total surface area of the capillary wall in the rete of the eel is about $105\,\mathrm{m}^2$ although the volume of blood in the rete is less than a drop—only $0.064\,\mathrm{cm}^3$. So there is a very large ratio of diffusion area to blood volume in the rete; around $1\,700\,\mathrm{m}^2 : 1\,\mathrm{cm}^3$, nearly 20 times greater than that in human lungs.

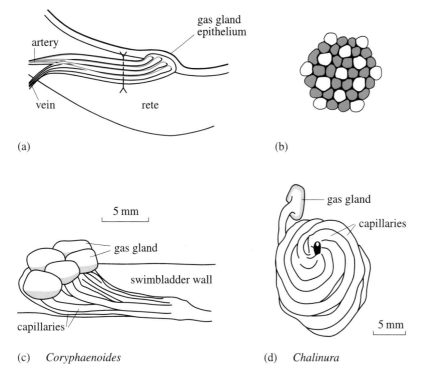

(a)

(b)

(c)   *Coryphaenoides*

(d)   *Chalinura*

Figure 4.9   (a) A detailed diagram of the rete mirabile and gas gland. (b) A cross-sectional view of the rete at the position shown by the vertical line in Figure 4.9a. Arterial capillaries are shown in blue. The retia of two deep-sea fish, (c) *Coryphaenoides* and (d) *Chalinura*, showing the enormous length of the capillaries.

The general blood (systemic) circulation is linked to the swimbladder at the gas gland via the rete (see Figure 4.8a), but there is also a second connection without the intervention of a rete. In closed swimbladders (Figure 4.8b), this second connection is at a special region which can be sealed off from the rest of the swimbladder by sphincter muscles. Because of its shape, this region is known as the oval. Sometimes (as in wrasse) a transverse septum with a hole surrounded by a sphincter muscle divides the portion of the swimbladder connected with the systemic circulation from the main region. In some open swimbladders (as in the eel, Figure 4.8a), this connection is found on the pneumatic duct.

4.3.3 Operation of the swimbladder

Let us now consider the way in which fish solve the three problems they face when changing depth.

1   How is gas lost from the swimbladder as the fish ascends?

This problem is the easiest to solve. Because the blood in the systemic circulation will have a P_{O_2} of around 20 kPa, all that is required to lose gas from the swimbladder is to arrange a connection between the swimbladder and the circulation, and to ensure that this connection can be shut off when no more gas is to be lost. As we have seen, in closed swimbladders, this connection is provided by the oval (Figure 4.8b), and in open swimbladders, by the pneumatic duct (Figure 4.8a). In fish such as conger eels, a decrease in ambient pressure first causes the swimbladder to swell, which opens the sphincter to the pneumatic duct and gas diffuses into the systemic circulation at the network of vessels that connect with the wall of the duct. If the ambient pressure decreases further, gas is belched out via the oesophageal sphincter.

There is, however, a definite limit to the rate at which fish with closed swimbladders can lose gas as they ascend in the water. For example, experiments on cod which had been adapted to different initial pressures and then subjected to reduced pressures, showed that they can lose 12–36 cm^3 gas $kg^{-1} h^{-1}$. The greater the pressure to which the cod was adapted beforehand, the greater was the rate of loss of gas from the swimbladder. After reading the next section, you should be able to see why the initial pressure to which the cod were adapted made a difference to the rate of loss of gas.

2   How is gas prevented from diffusing out of the swimbladder?

This second problem is solved in a most ingenious way. Next time you buy a fish (not a mackerel or a flatfish such as plaice) for supper, open the visceral cavity and expose the internal organs; the swimbladder is usually conspicuous because it is silvery even if it is not full of gas. The silvery layer on the swimbladder is formed by a series of thin overlapping platelets of guanine about 3 μm thick which make the bladder impermeable. Eric Denton of the Marine Biological Association Laboratory at Plymouth showed (using an isolated swimbladder from a conger eel) that if the silvery layer was removed there was a rapid loss of gas from the bladder. This loss of gas takes place by diffusion, and the impermeability of the silvery layer results from the great length of the diffusion pathway from the inside to the outside, which is formed by the overlapping, impermeable, guanine platelets. This is a beautiful solution to the problem of constructing an elastic impermeable bladder from natural material because, provided that the platelets are numerous and of sufficient size, they remain impermeable even if the walls of the swimbladder are stretched and shrunk as the fish alters its depth in the water. Conger eels do not live at great depths, and the swimbladder is made sufficiently impermeable by a relatively thin layer of guanine crystals. However, in deep-sea fish, where the problem of preventing gas diffusing from the swimbladder is much greater, the guanine platelet layer is about ten times thicker, and the swimbladders look much more silvery than those of shallow-water fish.

At the gas gland, systemic blood must be brought into contact with the swimbladder to enable the secretion of gas, so a potential leak must exist here. Why does gas not diffuse out of the swimbladder into the circulation at this point as it is arranged to do at the oval? The answer to this question is that it does and it doesn't! Consider the arrangement of the rete mirabile, with its incoming and outgoing capillaries closely apposed in parallel. If there is any difference in P_{O_2} between outgoing and incoming capillaries, oxygen diffuses across from one to the other. Suppose that oxygen diffuses out of the swimbladder into the outgoing venous capillaries at the gas gland and raises the blood P_{O_2}. Oxygen will then diffuse from the venous capillaries across into the incoming arterial capillaries along the length of the rete, so that blood finally leaves the rete (if the rete is long enough) with a P_{O_2} very nearly the same as that of the incoming blood at the beginning of the rete. In other words, the P_{O_2} along the outgoing capillary drops while that in the incoming capillary rises; little, if any, oxygen would be lost from the swimbladder. This ingenious counter-current arrangement effectively prevents any loss of gas from the swimbladder, as summarized in Figure 4.10.

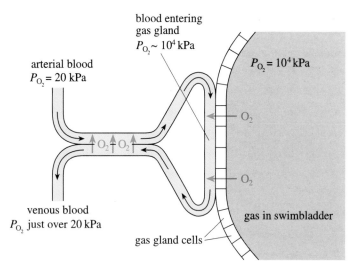

Figure 4.10   How the rete mirabile prevents loss of gas from the swimbladder. Oxygen dissolves in the blood passing through the gas gland but very little of it escapes from the swimbladder because it is 'short-circuited' by the counter-current system of the rete.

The greater the depth at which the fish normally lives, the greater is the difference in partial pressure between the swimbladder gases and the gases in the surrounding seawater and systemic circulation. It is not surprising then that not only the thickness of the guanine crystal layer, but also the length and complexity of the retial system (Figure 4.9c, d) is greater when this partial pressure gradient is greater. The longest retia yet found occur in the deep-sea fish; in some cases they are 60 mm long. This length is amazing—normal capillaries in muscle are only around 0.5 mm long.

3   How is gas secreted into the swimbladder as the fish descends?

This problem proved to be much more of a puzzle to physiologists than the two we have already considered. It had long been obvious that the retia were involved, and that there must be some change in the blood as it flows through the gas gland into the wall of the swimbladder. What is needed is a way of reducing the amount of gas in the venous blood leaving the rete to a level that is lower than that in the arterial blood entering the rete. The reduction (i.e. the difference in the amount of gas between the two) need not be very great, for the counter-current mechanism of the rete is designed to multiply small effects. A moment's reflection suggests that the process must rely on some rather special property of the blood, for if the partial pressure of the gas in the venous capillaries of the rete (i.e. after gas has been secreted into the swimbladder) is lower than that in the incoming arterial capillaries, we should expect gas to diffuse across from the arterial to the venous side of the rete, and the whole process of secretion would grind, or rather diffuse, to a halt. As we have seen, the gas secreted in almost all fish is oxygen, so we need to look for some special properties of the blood with respect to its oxygen content.

At this point, we need to be clear about the distinction between the total oxygen content of blood and the oxygen partial pressure (P_{O_2}). The amount of oxygen held by haemoglobin is dependent upon the partial pressure of oxygen—a relationship expressed by the oxygen dissociation curve. However, the oxygen content of blood (measured as vol%) comprises both oxygen bound to haemoglobin and an amount of oxygen present in simple physical solution, which varies according to the oxygen partial pressure. *Diffusion of oxygen occurs down a gradient of partial pressure rather than a gradient of oxygen content.* What is needed therefore is some method of raising the P_{O_2} of the oxygen in the blood as it passes through the gas gland and back into the rete, while at the same time lowering the actual oxygen content. In this way, oxygen will diffuse across into the swimbladder and from the venous to the arterial capillaries in the rete.

An important clue as to how the system operates comes from measurements of the effects of lowered pH on the oxygen dissociation curve of fish blood. These show that the acidification of mammalian blood causes a shift in the dissociation curve to the right. This Bohr shift reduces the affinity of haemoglobin for oxygen, but if the P_{O_2} is high, even highly acidified haemoglobin (or haemoglobin exposed to a high P_{CO_2}) can eventually become fully saturated with oxygen (Figure 4.11a). Haemoglobins displaying a Bohr effect have a reduced affinity for oxygen on acidification, but the amount of oxygen bound when the pigment is fully saturated (i.e. the oxygen-carrying capacity) is unaffected. The blood of most teleost fish responds to acidification in a rather different and more striking way. Not only is the dissociation curve affected, but the total oxygen-carrying capacity of the pigment is greatly changed by acidity. Even at a very high P_{O_2}, the acidified pigment fails to attain full saturation. This effect is illustrated in Figure 4.11b and is termed the **Root effect**. The important implication is that if the blood is acidified (e.g. by lactic acid or by an increase in P_{CO_2}) then, even at the very high oxygen partial pressures near an oxygen-containing swimbladder of a fish at depth, the haemoglobin may be incompletely saturated.

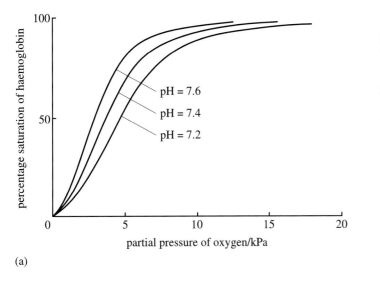

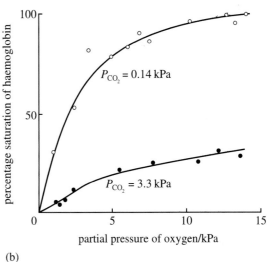

(a)

(b)

Figure 4.11 (a) The Bohr effect, where an increased acidity of the blood reduces the affinity of the pigment for oxygen (i.e. the curve shifts to the right). (b) The Root effect, shown in the oxygen dissociation curve of the sea robin (*Prionotus carolinus*). Modest partial pressures of carbon dioxide are sufficient to prevent the full loading of the pigment, even when the partial pressure of O_2 is high.

Elegant experiments on fish that live in shallow water, in particular studies by Berg, Steen and colleagues on eels, have shown how the Root effect contributes to the secretion of gas into the swimbladder. In most fish with open swimbladders, there is little or no gas secretion, and gas is gained by swallowing at the surface. However, the eel has a rather atypical open swimbladder and secretes gas. Berg and Steen succeeded in the extremely delicate task of removing small samples of venous and arterial blood by cannulation of the vessels just next to an active rete. They found that blood leaving the gas gland has a lower pH and a higher lactic acid content than has blood entering the gland, suggesting lactic acid is secreted by the glandular epithelium of the gas gland. The gas gland cells are rich in glycogen, and in the enzymes carbonic anhydrase and lactate dehydrogenase, and they release lactic acid into the hairpin end loops of the rete as they pass the gland. The acidification of blood produces a significant Root effect: when fully saturated haemoglobin arrives at the gas gland and its pH is lowered, a significant amount of bound oxygen is released from the haemoglobin, even though the ambient partial pressure of oxygen is high. This extra oxygen in solution increases the partial pressure of oxygen in the blood still further. Blood leaving the gas gland therefore has a higher partial pressure of oxygen than blood entering the gland, and in the rete oxygen therefore diffuses from venous to arterial blood.

Lactic acid has another important effect. An increased concentration of any solute decreases the solubility of any gas in solution. (The absorption coefficients of oxygen decrease with increasing salinity, which explains why saltwater has a lower oxygen content than freshwater at the same partial pressure.) The addition of lactic acid to the blood passing through the gas gland therefore decreases the solubility of oxygen, which causes the P_{O_2} to increase. This **salting-out** effect influences the solubility of all dissolved gases, which may account for the high partial pressure of nitrogen in the swimbladders of some deep-sea fish. Theoretical grounds seemed to suggest that salting-out would deposit gas only at a very low rate, and also could not raise the partial pressure of swimbladder gases to more than about 10^3 kPa, well below the measured values of about 10^4 kPa. However, more recent calculations indicate that salting-out effects may be more significant than originally supposed.

We now know that the major factor that elevates the P_{O_2} in the blood near the gas gland depends upon the unique loop-like arrangement of the capillaries of the rete and gas gland. Figure 4.12a shows diagrammatically how a single capillary forms a 'hairpin loop' near the gas gland epithelium. We already know that lactic acid raises the partial pressure of oxygen in the blood passing through the gas gland both by the Root effect and by salting-out. This increased P_{O_2} can be termed for convenience the 'primary effect'. Consequently, there is diffusion of oxygen from venous to arterial blood of the rete. Thus, the blood now entering the gas gland via the arterial capillaries will have a P_{O_2} greater than 20 kPa (see Figure 4.12b) and, when this blood in turn is acidified, the P_{O_2} in the blood adjacent to the gas gland increases still further. Because the P_{O_2} of the blood in the venous capillary is always greater than the P_{O_2} of the blood in the arterial capillary, free oxygen is constantly returned to the arterial capillary and the hairpin loop accumulates oxygen in the end of the rete nearest the gas-gland epithelium (Figure 4.12c). Thus the primary effect is multiplied in the presence of counter-current flow to produce a modest P_{O_2} gradient across the rete, from the venous to the arterial side, and a very substantial gradient along the length of the capillary vessels (Figure 4.12d). This process of **counter-current multiplication** means that the rete has the potential to accumulate oxygen in the blood entering the gas gland to very high levels (Figure 4.12e).

But there is one potential snag in the system. The capillary walls of the rete are permeable to lactic acid, which (along with the oxygen and ions) tends to diffuse across from the venous to the arterial side of the rete. The loss of lactic acid by

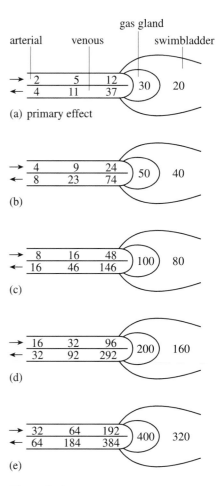

Figure 4.12   Counter-current multiplication using imaginary figures for oxygen partial pressure at different points along the rete, at the gas gland, and in the swimbladder. (a) shows the primary effect, based on measured data, which is multiplied in steps (b)–(e). (For convenience, partial pressures of oxygen are expressed in 10^4 Pa, i.e. in (a) the P_{O_2} is $2 \times 10^4 = 20$ kPa.)

diffusion means that as the blood flows away from the gas gland and through the rete, it becomes progressively more alkaline, so haemoglobin begins to pick up oxygen again and become fully saturated. Why does this process not have the disastrous effect of increasing the oxygen content of the blood leaving the rete, thus reducing the amount of oxygen available for secretion in the swimbladder? The important point is that the half-time of the loading of the haemoglobin with oxygen following increased alkalinity (the Root-on effect) is slow (10–20 s) compared with unloading in response to increased acidity (the Root-off effect), which takes only 50 ms. The free oxygen molecules can therefore recombine with haemoglobin to only a small extent before the outgoing blood has left the rete, provided that the flow rate of blood through the rete is sufficiently high. This process ensures that the outgoing blood of the rete contains less oxygen in chemical combination than does the incoming blood, although the partial pressures of the incoming and outgoing bloods (and their acidity) may be almost identical. The difference in oxyhaemoglobin content of the two bloods represents the oxygen available for secretion into the swimbladder. Counter-current multiplication in the rete permits the build-up of free oxygen at the gas gland until a diffusion of the gas can occur from the gland into the lumen of the swimbladder.

There is general agreement amongst physiologists who have studied swimbladder gas secretion, that the scheme briefly summarized above, worked out by experiments on shallow-water fish, must in essence, be applicable also to deep-sea fish. But the relative importance of the Root shift and the salting-out effect is still uncertain for deep-sea fish, and some puzzles remain. First, at oxygen tensions above 40×10^2 kPa (i.e. a depth of around 400 m) not all deep-sea fish show a Root shift when their blood is acidified, so the salting–out effect seems the more important. Second, the multiple retia (Figure 4.9) of many deeper-living fish seem to be devices for ensuring slow blood flow through the retia and hence, even if there is a Root shift, it would seem that the Root-on shift would occur within the retia, just what is not wanted. Perhaps flow within the venous capillaries of the rete is more rapid than in the arterial capillaries as they are often much larger than the arterial capillaries and offer less resistance to flow.

For obvious reasons, we know little about the rates of gas secretion in deep-sea fish. However, it is easy to measure how fast secretion takes place in fish living in shallower water. Simple experiments in which fish were subjected to pressure increases which decreased the volume of the swimbladder, and were then left to secrete gas until neutral buoyancy was achieved again, showed that fish with closed swimbladders such as cod (*Gadus morhua*) and saithe (*Pollachius virens*), could secrete around 1.5 cm^3 kg^{-1} body weight h^{-1}, whilst eels (*Anguilla*) and goldfish (*Carassius auratus*) with open swimbladders secreted gas at around one-quarter of this rate. So gas secretion is relatively slow, much slower than gas resorption.

4.3.4 Swimbladders and habitats

Quite a large number of teleost fish have reduced swimbladders or none at all, and are always negatively buoyant. This situation seems very curious, considering the advantages of neutral buoyancy conferred by gas-filled swimbladders. Because the problems of gas secretion and retention become more severe the deeper a fish lives, we might not unreasonably guess that fish with gas-filled swimbladders would be rare in the deep sea. However, Marshall, who has greatly increased our knowledge of the structure and function of swimbladders in marine fish, has shown that swimbladders are found in fish living near the bottom of oceans, even at great depths. However, generally they are reduced or absent in fish that live near the surface, (though some fish near the surface have them) and they are absent from many fish living at moderate depths (Figure 4.13).

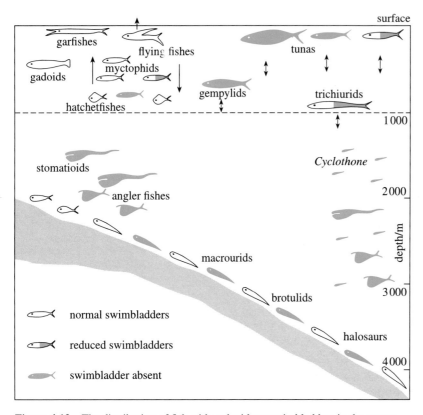

Figure 4.13   The distribution of fish with and without swimbladders in the oceans. Arrows indicate groups that show vertical migrations.

If fish normally rest on the sea bottom, as do flatfish such as plaice (*Pleuronectes platessa*), it is unnecessary for them to be neutrally buoyant, and such fish have no swimbladders. Increased density is probably advantageous in preventing them being swept along by currents. Similarly, in fast-flowing freshwater streams, many fish reduce the volume of their swimbladders in order to be negatively buoyant, and so avoid being swept downstream. For example, the darter (*Percina*) in rapid streams, has no gas in its swimbladder. On the other hand, fish that seek their food by slowly cruising or hovering just off the bottom need to be neutrally buoyant, as is the darter in slow streams (where its swimbladder is full of gas). Even at great depths, where the problems of gas secretion and retention are very severe, there are fish with swimbladders (such as macrourids) living near the bottom. We know from photographs and videos taken from deep sea vehicles, that macrourids do in fact cruise slowly around just off the sea bottom.

Near the surface, where gas secretion and retention pose fewer problems than in the deep sea, we might expect that all bony fish would have swimbladders to provide neutral buoyancy. Of course, some do (Figure 4.13). It turns out, when we look at these, that they are all fish which live close to the surface, such as flying fish or garfish, and these have swimbladders comprising the usual 5% of the fish's volume. However, fast-swimming fish, such as mackerels or tunas living mainly near the surface, have either reduced the swimbladder to only 2% of the fish's volume, or they have lost it altogether.

■ Why do these fish forego the advantages of neutral buoyancy?

Unlike flying fish, they move up and down in the upper layers of the sea, and part of the answer lies in what happens as they change depth.

Remembering that for every 10 m depth increase in the oceans, ambient pressure increases by 101.3 kPa, you can see that a change in depth from the surface to 10 m doubles ambient pressure from atmospheric pressure of 101.3 kPa to 202.6 kPa and, if such fish had a swimbladder, its volume would be halved. So, near the surface, fairly small changes in depth have large effects on the volume of the swimbladder and on the buoyancy of the fish. The deeper the fish normally lives, the less significant will be the effect of such small changes in depth. For example, a fish living at 400 m that moved down to 410 m would experience a change in ambient pressure of 101.3 kPa. This increase is only 2.5% of the ambient pressure at 400 m (4052 kPa), and would cause a decrease in swimbladder volume of 2.5%, which would have only a marginal effect on the fish's buoyancy. The inevitable large changes in volume as fish change depth near the surface, suggest that a swimbladder is not well suited to be a buoyancy device there, but this is not the whole answer to why fish such as mackerels and tunas have lost it. We saw earlier that most pelagic sharks are not neutrally buoyant, and that the extra drag associated with lift generation becomes less significant the faster the fish swims. It is because tunas and mackerels are designed for fast swimming that they can 'afford' to be negatively buoyant.

A good many different kinds of fish with swimbladders make regular vertical migrations. The champion migrators are probably the little myctophid lantern fish, some of which rise to the surface at night, and return at dawn to their daytime depths of 200–300 m. Larger fish, such as saithe, move to the surface at night from a daytime depth of 100 m or so. Cod and herring move less spectacular distances, but enough to experience significant changes in ambient pressure. Gas secretion and resorption are much too slow to cope with the speed of the depth changes of fish like myctophids, and they are too slow for cod and saithe as well. After an increase in ambient pressure equivalent to a move from the surface to a 10 m depth, saithe take 24 hours to compensate by restoring the original swimbladder volume. When the pressure change is reversed, it takes only 5 hours for the resorption of gas to occur. So fish which make these vertical migrations cannot be neutrally buoyant throughout their depth range. Curiously, the small *Myctophum punctatum* is almost always slightly negatively buoyant at the surface during the night, and is almost certainly negatively buoyant at depth during the day. Presumably, the access to a reliable source of food (copepod crustaceans) outweighs the extra energy cost of swimming (and perhaps escape from predators at the surface is important too).

Myctophids are small oceanic fish, and so not easy to study. We know much more about buoyancy changes with depth in cod, thanks to interesting work recently published by the Lowestoft Fisheries Laboratory. 300 kHz ultrasound tags were fitted to cod, which could then be tracked continuously by sector-scanning sonar for up to 2 days, as they swam freely up and down in the North Sea. The fish were either released at the surface or from a cage on the bottom where they had been kept for some time to adapt to ambient pressure. Figure 4.14a and b shows two of the results obtained. In the first (Figure 4.14a), the cod released at the surface made a rapid dive and then returned near the surface, and thereafter steadily descended (apart from a short rest on the bottom in the early hours of the second morning). Presumably it was secreting gas throughout its gradual descent. The second fish adapted to the ambient pressure on the bottom (Figure 4.14b) and stayed there, making ascents well within the depth range with which it could cope (as shown by laboratory experiments). Most likely, cod are negatively buoyant and rest on the sea bottom, rising off it to feed, becoming near neutrally buoyant, but not exceeding its upper limit of swimbladder expansion (25%).

■   Why do you think that a herring chased by a cod could escape being eaten by swimming upwards?

Herring have open swimbladders and release gas via the anus as they ascend. This allows them to keep the swimbladder volume and hence their density constant so that they are able rise directly from any depth to the surface without having to pause to equilibrate. The cod on the other hand, can only cope with changes in swimbladder volume of some 25%, which means that a cod adjusted for neutral buoyancy at 50 m could only rise to 37 m and still remain neutrally buoyant.

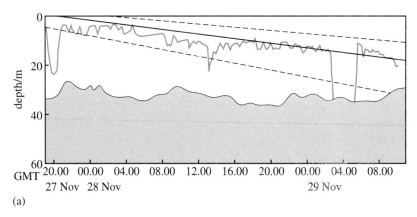

(a)

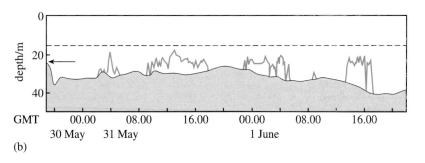

(b)

Figure 4.14   (a) The vertical track of a tagged cod released at the surface in the North Sea, and followed by sector-scanning sonar. After an initial dive and ascent, the cod slowly descended remaining within the dashed lines (which indicate the upper and lower limits of the range within which it could remain neutrally buoyant). The cod rested on the bottom (shown by the shaded area) near the end of the trace. (b) The vertical track of a second cod released from a cage on the bottom (at 24 m, indicated by the black arrow) where it had partially adapted to ambient pressure. The dashed line represents the upper limit at which it could have remained neutrally buoyant. This fish was probably negatively buoyant in water deeper than that at which it was released.

■ What are the advantages and disadvantages of different buoyancy mechanisms?

McNeill Alexander has sought to explain why fish adopt different kinds of buoyancy aids by calculating the metabolic costs of achieving buoyancy by swimbladders, by low-density fats and by fins. He began with the reasonable assumption that the mechanism favoured by evolution would be the one most economical of energy. For fish that swim at high speeds, dynamic lift from hydrofoil-like fins may involve the smallest metabolic cost. (Because the drag incurred in dynamic lift generation decreases as speed increases, it is in fact proportional to $1/v^2$.) Many of the teleost fish that swim all the time at high speeds lack swimbladders, e.g. mackerel and tunas. Likewise, for fast-swimming sharks, which lack swimbladders, we have already seen that hydrofoils are probably more economical than low-density lipids. Slow-moving sharks like the basking shark, however, need to have static lift from lipids.

For fish that do not cruise at high speeds, a swimbladder is probably the most economical means of avoiding sinking. But, for fish such as the many myctophids that make large daily vertical migrations, swimbladders filled with gas seem less economical than those filled with lipids. In fact, there is quite a good correlation between the amount of lipid in the swimbladders of different myctophids and the extent of their vertical migrations. However, swimbladders have important secondary functions that may outweigh some of the energetic disadvantages in vertically migrating fish. The swimbladder plays an important role in hearing in several fish groups, including the herring-like fish, and in the production of sound, in which the swimbladder may act as an important resonator. Some of these other functions may be impaired when the swimbladder volume changes as the fish undergoes extensive vertical migrations and more attention should be paid to its additional roles, particularly in deep-sea fish and the many species that undergo vertical migrations. Fish with swimbladders are about twice as sensitive to external pressure changes than have fish without them, and they can detect changes of around 0.5%. Stretch receptors in the swimbladder wall are thought to be involved, firing at different rates according to the changes in swimbladder volume resulting from pressure changes.

There is still much that we do not know about swimbladders, and if the reader is still pondering why it is that the swimbladders of fish undertaking vertical migrations are not designed like that of the eel or herring, i.e. with the possibility of rapid loss of gas on ascent as a safety measure against being swept to the surface, you may feel encouraged to know that so too are all fish physiologists who have considered the matter!

Summary of Section 4.3

Because of its very low density, gas offers a greater amount of upthrust per unit of volume, so modest amounts of gas can provide fish with sufficient lift. But if a fish with a gas-filled swimbladder is to retain neutral buoyancy at a range of depths, some mechanism must enable the mass of gas in the swimbladder to be altered so that the total volume is kept constant. Reducing the mass of gas is relatively easy because gas is lost into the general circulation via the oval (in closed swimbladders) or the pneumatic duct (in open swimbladders). Gas is retained in the closed swimbladder and in that of the eel by an enveloping layer of guanine, and by a rete mirabile, composed of closely juxtaposed venous and arterial capillaries. The rete also enables gases, including oxygen, to be secreted into the lumen of the swimbladder via the gas gland. Because of the Root effect, acidification of the blood at the gas gland readily results in unloading of oxyhaemoglobin, even when the ambient P_{O_2} is very high. (The reverse process of loading when the pH rises is relatively slow.) The 'hairpin' counter-current arrangement of capillaries tends to accumulate oxygen within the capillaries until a substantial gradient of oxygen partial pressure is established along the length of the rete. The addition of lactic acid also increases the partial pressure of gases by salting-out. These processes are sufficient to add gas to the swimbladder against substantial gradients of partial pressure. Note, however, that although gas secretion is understood in general terms, some puzzles concerning gas secretion in deep-sea fish still remain.

4.4 Conclusion

Most fish are more dense than the water in which they swim, and they have to generate dynamic lift by using outspread pectorals as lifting foils. This process generates drag, and hence increases the energy of such fish. One way in which fish can reduce the muscular energy expenditure required to maintain their station in water is to store sufficient low-density material which makes them the same density as water. Fish use quite different materials to provide static lift. Gas is efficient in providing lift, since its density is low, and many teleosts possess gas-filled swimbladders. However, some fish, including some deep-sea species, have replaced gas with lipid. Although lipid is a lot bulkier than gas, it has the advantage that the lift provided varies little with depth because changes in ambient pressure have relatively little effect on the volume of lipid. The fact that many mid-water fish species that undergo substantial vertical migrations use lipid as a source of static lift probably reflects the difficulties of regulating buoyancy with a gas-filled bladder over a wide range of depths.

Objectives for Chapter 4

After completing Chapter 4 you should be able to:

4.1 Define and use, or recognize definitions and applications of, each of the **bold** terms.

4.2 Explain the advantages of neutral buoyancy, and outline the advantages and drawbacks of using lipid or using gas in a flexible bag as a source of static lift.

4.3 Draw diagrams to show the structure of open and closed swimbladders.

4.4 Explain the mechanism by which gas is secreted into the swimbladder.

4.5 Explain the role of the swimbladder in species that migrate vertically and describe any additional functions the swimbladder may have.

Questions for Chapter 4

(Answers to questions are at the end of the book.)

Question 4.1 (Objectives 4.1–4.5)

For each of the following statements, decide whether the statement is true or false and explain why.

(a) The amount of lift generated by a swimbladder full of oxygen is not influenced by the depth at which the fish is swimming.

(b) If a fish is more dense than seawater, a considerable part of its propulsive power may go towards maintaining its level in the water.

(c) No known fish has the ability to contain gas within a rigid chamber, where the volume does not change as ambient pressure alters.

(d) Unless the total volume of its swimbladder is kept constant, the overall density of a fish will increase as it moves down deeper in the sea.

(e) Because oxygen has to be moved into the swimbladder against substantial gradients of partial pressure, oxygen is transported by active processes that require ATP.

(f) In all fish with open swimbladders, the sphincter muscle at the oval may regulate the extent to which oxygen is added to the bladder.

(g) Those fish that demonstrate daily vertical migrations in the sea are likely to move up or down slowly, and this allows compensatory resorption or secretion of oxygen to maintain neutral buoyancy.

(h) Some of the non-buoyancy functions of a swimbladder might be impaired if its volume were to change during vertical migration.

Question 4.2 (Objectives 4.2 and 4.4)

Provide an explanation in physiological terms for the following observations (a–g).

(a) The amount of guanine present in the wall of the swimbladder is greatest in fish that live at substantial depths and least in those that live near the surface.

(b) The rete associated with the gas gland in deep-sea fish is unusually long compared to that of fish from shallower waters.

(c) Gas-gland tissue shows a very high activity of glycolytic enzymes, especially lactate dehydrogenase.

(d) Some freshwater fish have closed swimbladders that are filled almost entirely with nitrogen.

(e) The concentration of carbon dioxide within the swimbladder is usually close to zero.

(f) There is a gradient of lactate along the rete of *Anguilla* in both the arterial capillaries conveying blood to the gas gland and in the venous capillaries conveying blood away. For both types of capillary, there is a higher lactic acid content at the end of the vessel nearer the gas gland.

(g) As a general rule, lipid stores are used as a source of static lift much more by marine fish than by freshwater species.

From the following statements (a–i), referring to the operation of counter-current multiplication in the swimbladder, identify the four that are true, and then place them in the appropriate chronological order in which they occur, starting with (a), (b) or (c).

(a) Blood from the heart eventually arrives at the far end of the rete with a P_{O_2} of 200 kPa, and with most of the oxygen contained in the blood present in simple physical solution.

(b) The haemoglobin begins to unload oxygen at the oval, and the relaxation of the sphincter muscle ensures that the unloaded oxygen passes into the swimbladder.

(c) The blood arriving at the rete has a partial pressure of about 20 kPa, most of the oxygen in it is bound as oxyhaemoglobin and its concentration of lactic acid is only slightly higher than in the systemic circulation.

(d) Oxygen that at an earlier stage was unloaded from haemoglobin now starts to recombine with it as the pH increases, although this happens relatively slowly.

(e) Lactic acid passes into the blood from the gas gland, but, because of the Root effect, the partial pressure of oxygen in the blood remains unchanged until counter-current multiplication begins.

(f) The pH of the blood passing towards the gas gland decreases because of inward diffusion of lactic acid, and the P_{O_2} therefore begins to increase.

(g) The addition of lactic acid to the blood at this point has the effect of increasing the solubility of the gases in the plasma, although this has no effect on the partial pressure of the gas.

(h) The oxygen partial pressure in the arterial capillaries of the rete now begins to increase because of diffusion of oxygen from the venous capillaries.

(i) As the venous blood is leaving the rete capillaries, it has a P_{O_2} that is approximately the same as that of the blood entering the rete (20 kPa), but its oxygen content is much higher.

Explain, in physiological terms, the following generalizations:

(a) Many of the teleosts that inhabit the upper layers of the sea tend not to have a swimbladder, unless they live exclusively just at the surface.

(b) Many (but not all) of the deep-sea teleosts lack a swimbladder or have a swimbladder filled with lipid rather than gas.

CHAPTER 5   PRINCIPLES OF FLIGHT

Prepared for the Course Team by David Robinson

5.1 Introduction

The study of flight in animals owes much to the work carried out on human- or machine-powered flight, but there has been relatively little information transfer in the other direction. Indeed, one of the surprising facts about the early pioneers of aviation is how little they drew on observations of flying animals, in pursuing their goal of human flight. One of the saddest clips of archive film of early aviators, shows a man at the top of the Eiffel Tower in Paris wearing a coat with extended arms that were intended to resemble the wings of birds. As he attempts to fly off the top of the tower, gravity takes over and he plummets to his death. The fact that the wings of birds are large relative to their body size should have challenged his confidence in his small wings. Did he really believe that he could flap his arms so powerfully with his muscles that he could maintain powered flight? As you read through this chapter and the next you will encounter the anatomical and physiological adaptations that enable birds and some other animals to fly and, in doing so, will appreciate why the early dream that humans could fly with wings strapped to their arms was always an impossible one.

There are significant parallels between the study of the mechanics of swimming in fish and the study of the aerodynamics of flight in birds, and there has been considerable cross-fertilization of ideas and techniques amongst researchers. However, although both swimming and flying involve moving through a three-dimensional medium, water and air respectively, water is much more viscous than air and is almost incompressible. In the earlier chapters of this book you have read about the mechanics of swimming in fish and the problems of maintaining position in the water against a gravitational force. In this chapter the principles of flight will be introduced, using birds as an example. Chapter 6 considers the application of these principles to a variety of other animal groups.

It is inevitable that much of the study of animal flight has been carried out using birds. Birds are numerically a most successful group of vertebrates, with about 25 000 species and sub-species recognized so far, compared with some 15 000 mammals and a similar number of fish species. Figures for the number of species can rarely be given precisely. Despite the general lack of study of birds by early flight enthusiasts, there was one particular feature of birds that influenced the most scientific of the early workers on flight and that was the *shape* of the wing. It is the relationship between shape and aerodynamic performance that is explored in the next section.

5.2 The aerofoil

Otto Lilienthal spent 20 years working on flight in the late nineteenth century and he studied bird flight with the intention of producing a workable glider. The wing design that he developed had a gently curved upper surface. This subtle parabola gave the wing lifting power, according to Lilienthal, and was the key feature of a bird's wing that accounted for the **lift** (Chapter 2). The wingspan of his gliders was about 7 m, too small really from the aerodynamic point of view, but even so he made nearly 2 000 flights before crashing on 9th August 1896. He died one day later. His contribution to research on flight was the realization, from scientific observation, that a curved wing provided lift.

Prior to Lilienthal's work, wings were generally constructed as flat sheets. The flat sheet does provide some lift and a simple experiment will demonstrate this. Hold a piece of paper (about A4 size) in front of your mouth (Figure 5.1a) and blow across the upper surface. If you blow gently, the paper will gradually rise (Figure 5.1b, c). This experiment demonstrates one of the properties of wings—that if air flows faster over an upper surface, an upward force is generated.

A structure that generates lift is called an **aerofoil**. In the experiment with the paper, the lift was generated in an upward direction, but you should be aware that the force that generates lift does not necessarily act *vertically* upwards (Section 2.3.3).

5.2.1 An introduction to flight dynamics

If you look at a bird wing in the flight position, or at an aircraft wing, you will see that it is curved in cross-section. A typical bird wing section is shown in Figure 5.2a. When positioned in an air flow, the air that passes over the top of the wing section moves faster than that travelling below, as a consequence of the curved shape of the wing. The difference in speed produces a difference in pressure between the upper and lower surfaces. Thus, there is a vertical pressure gradient across the wing, with the higher pressure below, providing lift (Figure 5.2a, b). The larger the surface area over which the air flows, the greater the lift. You have read about the generation of hydrodynamic lift as a fish fin moves through water, in Section 2.3.3. In the fish fin, lift was only generated if there was an **angle of incidence** and if this angle was small. Similarly, in an aerofoil, lift is only generated in the presence of a small angle of incidence (typically −5° to +15°). At large angles of incidence the lift disappears.

■ Why does the lift decrease at large angles of incidence?

(a)

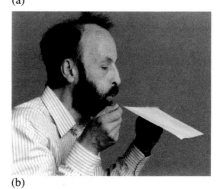
(b)

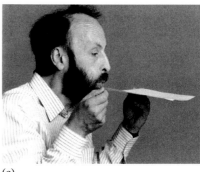
(c)

Figure 5.1 Blowing on a sheet of paper to demonstrate lift.

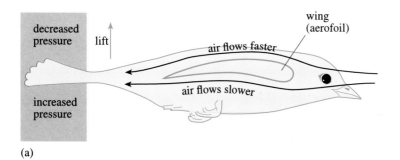
(a)

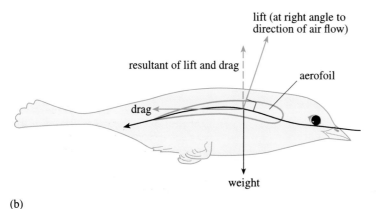
(b)

Figure 5.2 The air flow over an aerofoil. (a) The curvature (camber) of the wing alters the velocity of the air above the wing, creating a pressure gradient. (b) The forces generated on an aerofoil. The downward force due to gravity (the weight) is balanced by an upward force that is the resultant of lift and drag.

As you have read in Section 2.3.1, for the hydrofoil at small angles of incidence, the flow over an aerofoil is laminar (Figure 5.3a, b). As the angle of incidence increases (Figure 5.3b, c) the flow breaks up and spills off the upper surface of the aerofoil as turbulence. The velocity of the flow changes and the pressure gradient across the aerofoil is substantially reduced, leading to a loss of lift. At the point where the lift is so reduced that it does not counteract the gravitational force, the wing starts to fall and is said to have stalled. The optimum angle of incidence for an aerofoil is around 15°.

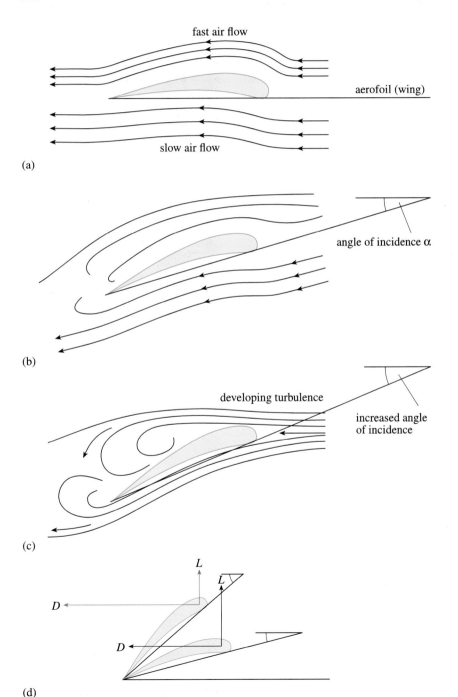

Figure 5.3 (a)–(c) The development of turbulent air flow across an aerofoil as the angle of incidence increases. (d) As the angle of incidence of the aerofoil increases, lift (*L*) decreases and drag (*D*) increases. The length of the arrows for *L* and *D* indicate the magnitude of these forces.

■   You should now be able to list three key factors that affect lift. What are they?

Three key factors that affect lift are:

(a) wing area (a);

(b) speed of air flow (v);

(c) angle of incidence (α).

The lift (L) that a wing can generate is derived from:

$$L \propto av^2$$

or $L = kav^2$

where k is a constant incorporating measures of the shape of the wing.

The maximum lift is generated at the optimum angle of incidence for the wing. The mass of the whole bird (or aircraft) divided by the total wing area gives the **wing loading** in $N\,m^{-2}$. Obviously the lift has to be greater than the downward force due to wing loading or the bird would not fly. The area of the wings is related to the size of the bird. A plot of the logarithm of wing loading against logarithm of body mass for a large number of bird species gives a strong positive correlation between the two parameters (Figure 5.4). So, although large birds have a greater wing area than small ones, their wing loading is greater. A consequence of this scale effect is that the minimum velocity of air over the wings necessary to provide sufficient lift for flight is higher in large birds than small ones. You can see this need for a higher air flow if you watch large birds take off from the ground. They have to run to build up speed before getting into the air, whereas small birds can just jump into the air and start flying. Of course a large bird may intentionally run into the wind, since it needs to maximize air flow across the wings, not its speed across the ground.

The shapes of bird wings vary substantially. In some species they are long and thin, like those of the albatross, while in others they are short and broad, like those of a pheasant. Two birds can have the same wing area, but very different wing shapes (Figure 5.5). Wing shape is defined by the **aspect ratio**, the ratio of the wing span to the chord (the mean distance between the leading and trailing edges of the wing). You should recall that an alternative method is used to calculate aspect ratio in the tail fin of a fish (Section 2.3.2):

aspect ratio = (span)^2 / surface area.

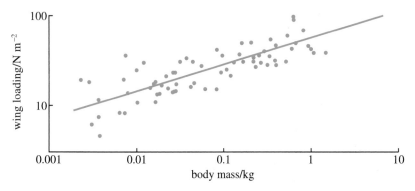

Figure 5.4   A plot of wing loading against body mass for 70 species of birds. Note that both axes are logarithmic.

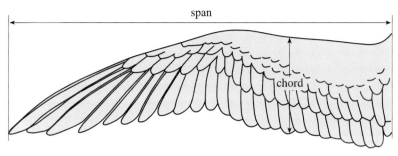

high aspect ratio

(a)

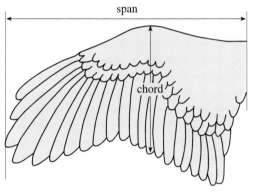

low aspect ratio

(b)

Figure 5.5 Two bird wings that have the same area but different aspect ratios. The two measurements that are made to calculate the aspect ratio are illustrated. Note that the span is a measurement made from wing-tip to body, not wing-tip to wing-tip. (a) A shearwater (*Puffinis puffinis*) wing; (b) a pheasant (*Phasianus colchicus*) wing.

There are some correlations between aspect ratio and the style of flight. In general, birds that glide or use high speed flight have wings with higher aspect ratios. Birds capable of a rapid take-off or of soaring on thermals generally have wings with low aspect ratios. Some reasons for these distinctions will become apparent when we consider soaring and gliding in Section 5.4.

Summary of Section 5.2

An aerofoil can generate lift and a bird's wing acts like an aerofoil. Three key factors influence the generation of lift: the area of the wing, the speed of the air flowing over it and the angle of incidence of the wing to the direction of air flow. The area of the wing is related to the size of the bird and larger birds have larger wings. However, the wing loading (mass of the bird divided by the total area of the wings) is greater in larger birds. The shape of the wings of a bird reflects its lifestyle. Wings can be short or long, broad or narrow, but the shape can be described by calculating the aspect ratio (the ratio of the wing span to the chord).

5.3 The forces acting on a bird in flight

Up to this point we have discussed the bird wing as if it were a static aerofoil like the wing of an aeroplane. However, the bird wing is only analogous to an aircraft wing in a bird that is gliding. Since power in a bird comes from movement of the wings, the aerodynamics become more complicated. Figure 5.6 shows the fundamental difference between the forces acting on a bird and those acting on an aircraft. As a bird flies through the air, it experiences a frictional drag due to the air flow over the body and a downward force due to the weight of the bird. Similar forces act on an aircraft but, in an aircraft they are counteracted by two separate forces: the lift derived from the wings and the forward thrust derived from the engine(s). In the bird, there is only one force: that provided from the wings, so the wings must beat such that the force developed (wingbeat in Figure 5.6b) has both a vertical component—lift—and a horizontal component—thrust. The wingbeat must counteract the weight, as well as providing forward movement.

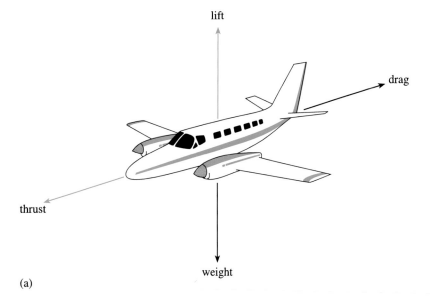

(a)

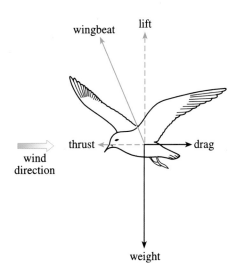

(b)

Figure 5.6 (a) The forces acting on an aeroplane in flight. (b) The forces acting on a bird in flight.

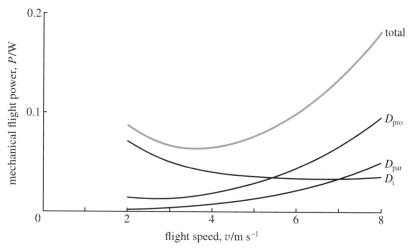

Figure 5.7 The variation of the components of mechanical power with flight speed in the swallow (*Hirundo rustica*). The total power output is shown, together with the proportions of that power used to overcome the three components of drag, D_{pro}, D_{par} and D_i.

Describing lift as an upward force is not strictly accurate since it makes the assumption that the bird is flying parallel to the ground. It may well not be, so the more accurate definition of **lift** is: that part of the force acting on a wing which is perpendicular to the direction of the air flow. **Drag** acts in the same direction as the air flow (Figure 5.2b). Both lift and drag increase with the speed of air flow, roughly according to the square law—that is, lift and drag are proportional to the square of the speed of air flow which is comparable to the situation of a fish in water (Section 2.3.1). Both also depend upon the size of the bird and the density of the air.

The force shown as drag in Figure 5.6 has three components. The frictional force on the body produces **parasite drag**, D_{par}, which is dependent upon the shape and size of the body. The drag that results from the air flow over the wings is called **profile drag**, D_{pro}, and it is influenced by the structure of the wings. The third component is **induced drag**, D_i, which is associated with the beating of the wings to generate lift. D_i, unlike D_{par} and D_{pro}, does *not* increase with the square of the speed, but is greatest at slow speeds close to stalling (Figure 5.7). We shall return to the phenomenon of induced drag in Section 5.7 in connection with wake analysis and vortex theory.

Most birds develop lift and thrust on the downstroke of the wing, flexing the wing on the upstroke to minimize D_{pro}. However, this is not the case for all birds. For example, the kestrel (*Falco tinnunculus*) generates lift on the upstroke also, which contributes to supporting its weight, but reduces the mean thrust. Analysis of the flight of birds in wind tunnels has shown that in small birds the upstroke—the 'return' stroke—generally has little or no aerodynamic effect. In the pigeon, for example, the wing tip is moved close to the body on the upstroke and only a small portion of each wing is in the air flow. This action reduces drag, but does not generate thrust or lift.

■ What is the consequence of this type of upstroke for the velocity of the bird?

If the upstroke does not generate lift or thrust, the bird decelerates during the upstroke. However, birds adapted for gliding may keep the wings extended during the upstroke in fast flight, generating lift. A bird that glides usually has thin wings with a high aspect ratio, factors that will give lower drag. For birds with a wing that produces high drag, generally the smaller birds and those with a low aspect ratio, the optimum strategy is to have a passive upstroke.

As you will read in Section 5.7, the differences between the wing movements of different species of bird have consequences for the air movements around these birds.

Summary of Section 5.3

The forces acting on a bird in flight are thrust, lift, drag and gravity. The wingbeat provides lift and also thrust for forward motion and the lift must counteract the force of gravity. Drag acts in the same direction as air flow and is divided into three components: parasite drag due to the shape and size of the body, profile drag due to the structure of the wings and induced drag due to the beating of the wings.

5.4 Soaring and gliding

Many large birds conserve energy by gliding, whenever wind conditions allow. In a glide, the bird holds its wings outstretched and descends relative to the direction of air flow. With a shallow angle of glide a bird can travel a considerable distance relative to the ground, particularly if it has started from a good height.

■   What other factors might affect gliding performance in a large bird?

Both wing loading and aspect ratio influence gliding performance. The speed of a glide depends on the wing loading, so generally a large bird travels faster than a small one and glides at a shallower angle. The angle is also dependent on the aspect ratio of the wing. A bird with a high-aspect-ratio wing, like the albatross (*Diomedea* sp.), can glide at a shallower angle than a vulture (e.g. *Gyps fulvus*), which has a lower aspect ratio.

The rate at which a bird descends is called the **sinking speed**. Measurements of sinking speed at different air speeds have shown that there are differences between species. The vulture has a minimum sinking speed of just under $2\,\mathrm{m\,s^{-1}}$ whereas for a pigeon the figure is $2.5\,\mathrm{m\,s^{-1}}$. By comparison, an aircraft built to glide can have a sinking speed of well under $1\,\mathrm{m\,s^{-1}}$.

■   Of the two birds mentioned above, the pigeon and the vulture, which would have the wings with the higher aspect ratio?

A high-aspect-ratio wing would be associated with good gliding ability and hence a slow sinking speed, so the vulture would have a higher aspect ratio wing than the pigeon.

5.4.1 Forces acting on a gliding bird

In Section 5.3 you considered the forces acting on a bird while it was flying. Obviously the forces acting on a gliding bird are similar, but the wing is held rigid. Figure 5.8 shows a gliding bird that is descending at an angle. The glide path is inclined to the horizontal so that the forward thrust is balanced by the drag. There is a vertical resultant force that counteracts the weight and the bird descends at a constant velocity and angle. If the glide path were rotated so that it was horizontal, then the lift would balance the weight and the bird would travel horizontally with a reducing velocity.

■   Why would the forward velocity decrease?

The drag would not be completely balanced by thrust, so velocity would decrease and, of course, the bird would be in a highly unstable state.

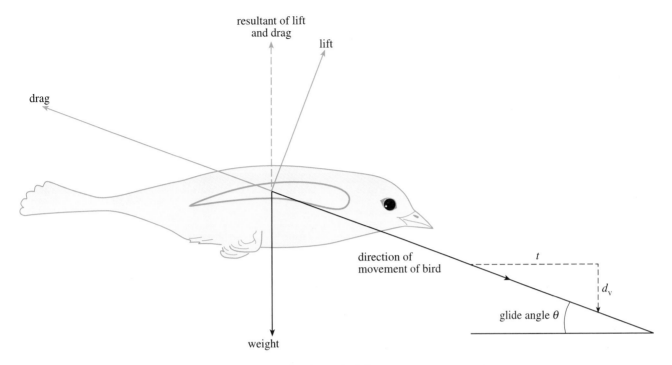

Figure 5.8   The forces acting on a gliding bird. Sinking speed = vertical distance moved / time taken (i.e. d_v / t).

Birds are able to change the characteristics of a glide. For example, at low speeds, the tail feathers are spread to increase lift. The vulture adjusts the angle of its body in the air, so changing the angle of descent. Then, as it approaches the ground, it extends its legs which act as brakes, steepening the angle of descent (Figure 5.9), and eventually lands on the ground. The mechanisms for altering the glide angle alter the glide distance. How then can some gliding birds apparently move horizontally or even rise?

5.4.2 Soaring on thermals

Hot air rises. Where there is uneven heating of air by the sun, for example on hillsides facing the sun, which are hotter than the surrounding land in shadow, warmer air rises, either as a column or a series of vortex rings. Such upward movements are called thermals. Gliding birds, by circling within the rising air use the lift that the air movement produces and glide upwards, or soar. Thermals over the plains of East Africa can rise as fast as $4\,\text{m s}^{-1}$.

■   What is the implication of the presence of thermals for a vulture gliding over the plains of East Africa?

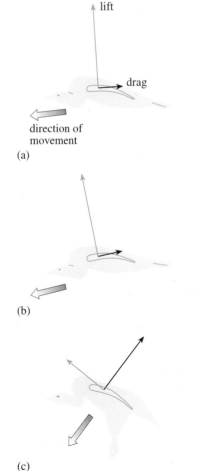

Figure 5.9   The vulture in gliding flight. (a) and (b) Tilting the body produces different gliding angles. (c) At any speed, the vulture can glide more steeply if the legs are lowered, acting as air brakes. The length of the lift and drag arrows indicates the magnitude of the force.

Figure 5.10   Slope soaring over a wave.

The vulture has a sinking speed of approximately $2\,\mathrm{m\,s^{-1}}$ (Section 5.4), so a thermal would provide a net gain in lift. Observations made on Ruepell's griffon vultures (*Gyps ruepellii*) over the Serengeti plains have shown that large distances can be travelled rapidly by soaring on a thermal and then gliding to the next. The vultures nest on cliffs at the edge of the plain and then travel to their feeding areas around the herds of mammals that inhabit the Serengeti. Colin Pennycuick of Bristol University followed the vultures in a motorized glider and discovered that one individual travelled 75 km in only 96 minutes entirely by using the thermals. The vultures can travel to great height on thermals, thus rising above the level of their cliff nest before returning from feeding.

■   Can you think of any limitations to soaring that would affect the vultures?

On cloudy days, and first thing in the morning, the vultures cannot go and feed because the temperatures are not high and hence not uneven enough to generate the thermals that they need.

5.4.3 Slope soaring

Rising air is also found over ridges—both ridges on land and waves on the sea. Sloping contours force wind upwards towards the ridge, it flows over the ridge and then rebounds. Over the long ocean stretches, the large waves can provide a whole series of rising and rebounding air currents that birds can utilize for soaring. The air currents do not give great vertical movement, unlike thermals, but they do still enable long distance travel because of their regular pattern (Figure 5.10).

Cliffs and sea margins also provide upward movement of air. Warm air flowing off the land rises over the cold air above the sea. Wind from the sea hitting the edge of a cliff is deflected upwards producing a localized, near vertical, air current—the obstruction current (Figure 5.11). The gannet (*Sula bassana*) shown in Plate 5.1 is gliding in the wind that blows almost continually around the Bass Rock in the Firth of Forth. The updraft is supporting the bird which, although moving relative to the air flow, appears almost stationary to an observer on the rock. Most birds that soar have prominent, separated feathers at the tips of their wings. These feathers spread out in both the vertical and horizontal plane. Their role appears to be to reduce drag.

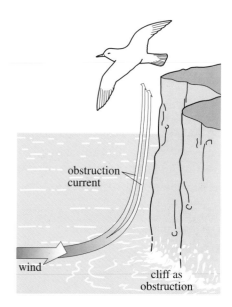

Figure 5.11   Obstruction currents at the edges of cliffs allow birds to gain height.

Summary of Section 5.4

Large birds can conserve energy by gliding, holding the wings outstretched. With the wings in this position, a bird will descend, its speed of descent being influenced by the wing loading and the aspect ratio of the wing. In regions where there are columns or patches of hot air rising, birds can glide upwards— soar—by circling within the rising air. The bird will rise providing that the air is rising faster than the bird's sinking speed in still air. Sloping ground or large ocean waves will deflect air upwards and birds can use this to rise, a strategy called slope soaring.

5.5 Structure of the bird wing

Birds first appeared in the fossil record during the Jurassic period 146–208 million years ago, evolving from the archosaurs, an ancient group of reptiles. The bird wing evolved from the front limb and so has similarities with the front limb of tetrapods such as reptiles and mammals. These similarities are apparent when a wing is compared with a human arm (Figure 5.12). Some of the bones are directly comparable, but from the wrist to the tip of the limb there is no immediate similarity. The birds evolved from reptiles which had a pentadactyl

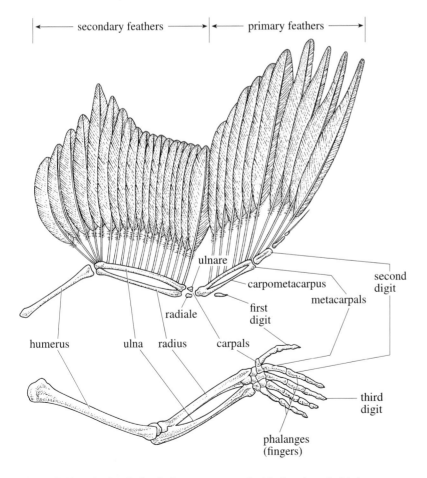

Figure 5.12   The forelimb of a human compared with the wing of a bird.

limb with five digits, so substantial fusion and loss of bones has occurred as evolution has progressed. In birds, there are two 'wrist' bones, a carpal at the end of the radius (the radiale) and one at the end of the ulna (the ulnare). The 'hand' has what appears to be a single bone made up from two that are fused at each end, the carpometacarpus. In fact, some interesting developmental studies have shown that this bone is formed from fusion of the carpals and metacarpals of three digits, equivalent to the first, second and third digit of the pentadactyl limb of the reptiles. The second digit is long and robust and carries feathers.

The numbering of the digits of the bird is a controversial area of research. It is possible that the bones of the digits found in birds are derived from the second, third and fourth digits of the pentadactyl limb, rather than the first, second and third. This debate is an important one for evolutionary biology, but of no direct aerodynamic significance.

The feathers on the bird wing probably evolved from the scales of reptiles, but the stages of evolution are not known. Wing feathers can be divided broadly into two types—flight and contour—based on their means of attachment to the wing.

Look at the wing in Figure 5.12. The flight feathers are inserted onto the ulna, the carpometacarpus and the second digit of the wing. Those on the ulna are the secondary flight feathers, and those on the carpometacarpus and second digit, the primaries. The ulna is thicker than the radius, to allow for the insertion of the tips of the flight feathers—a strong attachment is needed to withstand the forces acting on them during flight.

Over both surfaces of the wing are spread the contour feathers which give the wing its curved shape. The contour feathers have been removed from the wing illustrated in Figure 5.12. They are inserted onto the skin membrane that covers the wings, so contour feathers, unlike the flight feathers, do not have a firm base.

The first digit carries a small group of feathers which together form the alula or bastard wing (visible on the gannet in Plate 5.1). The alula has a limited amount of movement. It can be raised into the air flow over the wing to enhance lift as the wing approaches a stall. The laminar flow of the layers of air over the wing begins to break up as air speed drops or the angle of incidence increases; air flow becomes turbulent, lift declines and the wing can stall. When a bird raises the alula into the airstream, there is an increase in the velocity of the air travelling through the small gap between the alula and the main wing. This increase generates extra lift and the presence of the alula helps maintain laminar flow, so greater angles of incidence can be reached before stalling and greater lift is produced.

■   When might you see a bird with the alula raised into the airflow over its wing?

The alula is often used as birds land. At this stage in flight the bird is decelerating and there is a risk of stalling.

The structure of flight and contour feathers is compared in Figure 5.13. The interlocking barbs and barbules of the flight feathers produce a structure that is almost airtight, yet is light enough to remain firm while only attached to the wing at one end.

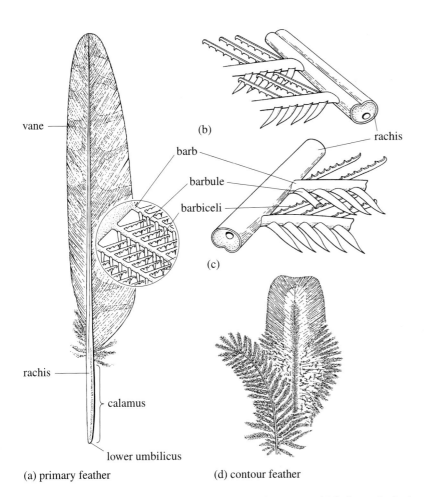

vane

(b)

rachis

barb

barbule

barbiceli

(c)

rachis

calamus

lower umbilicus

(a) primary feather

(d) contour feather

Figure 5.13   (a) A primary flight feather with an enlargement which shows the barbs.
(b) and (c) Magnified portions of the flight feather viewed from above (b) and below (c).
(d) A contour feather.

The flight feather (Figure 5.13a) is asymmetrical, with the rachis offset from the
centre (Figure 5.13a). This affects the behaviour of the feather during the
wingbeat cycle because the centre of pressure of the air is not along the line of
the stiffest part of the feather, the rachis. On the downstroke, the pressure acting
on the vane of the feather rotates it slightly about the point of insertion, forcing
the feathers on the wing together into a broad surface pushing against the air. On
the upstroke, the pressure acts on the feather in the opposite way, from the upper
surface, producing a twist in the other direction. The rotation opens gaps
between the feathers which reduces the resistance to air flow as the wing readies
itself for the next downward power stroke (Figure 5.14).

The bones of birds are much lighter than those of terrestrial vertebrates. The
lightening results from thinner walls and the lack of blood-forming or fatty
tissue filling the interior. To retain strength, the interior is stiffened with light
struts of bone (Figure 5.15).

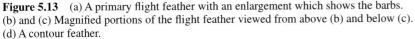

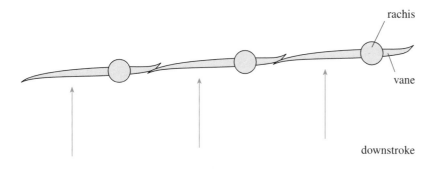

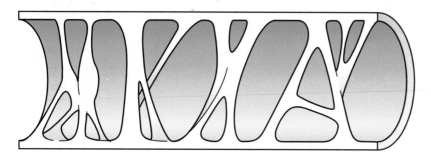

Figure 5.14   A cross-section through the feathers to show rotation during the wingbeat cycle. The arrows represent air movement.

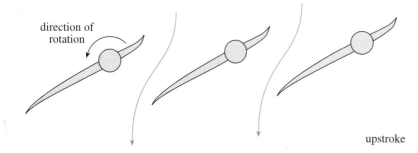

Figure 5.15   A longitudinal section through the humerus of a bird showing how the thin wall is strengthened by struts of bone. The cavities between the bone struts are filled with air.

Summary of Section 5.5

The structure of the bird wing is homologous with the structure of the typical tetrapod forelimb from which it evolved. The feathers on the wing are probably derived from the scales of reptiles, the group from which the birds diverged in the Jurassic period. The bones of birds are much lighter than those of terrestrial vertebrates. There are air-filled cavities within the bones and the walls of the bones are much thinner.

5.6 Flapping flight

In the introduction to this chapter you read about an early attempt by a man to fly from the Eiffel Tower using wings attached to his arms. The anatomical arrangement of muscles in the human does not allow the arms to generate sufficient power for flight. In birds, the anatomy of the pectoral girdle is highly modified and the muscles that move the wings are massive. Figure 5.16a shows the skeleton of a bird and Figure 5.16b the position of the flight muscles.

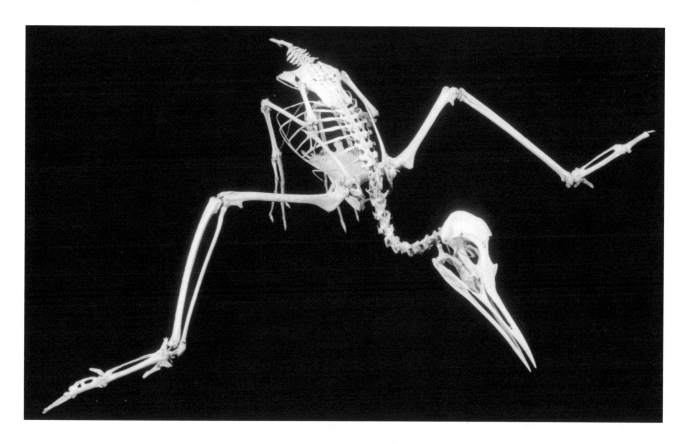

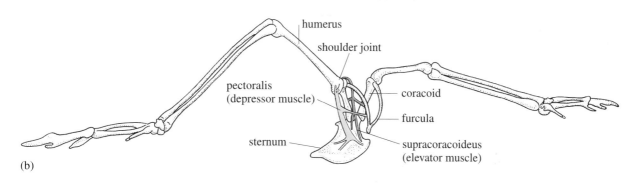

(b)

Figure 5.16 (a) Photograph of the skeleton of a common tern (*Sterno hirundo*) with the wings outstretched as in flight. (b) The attachments of the two major flight muscles to the skeleton (shown for one of the wings).

■   What is striking about the position of the muscles relative to the point of articulation of the wing?

Although the muscles raise and lower the wing, they lie *below* the point of articulation.

■   What is counter-intuitive about the muscle mass that raises the wing being below the point of articulation?

For a muscle to raise the wing it needs to pull the wing up and so needs to be above the wing or, to be more accurate, needs to exert a force on the upper surface of the wing. The muscle that raises the wing, the supracoracoideus (Figure 5.16b), has a long tendon that passes through a gap between the head of the humerus, the scapula and the coracoid bone. This gap is called the **foramen triosseum** . The tendon is attached to the deltoid ridge that runs along the dorsal surface of the humerus. Thus when the supracoracoideus contracts, the force is transmitted through the tendon and converted to an upward force on the humerus, so raising the wing. The system is just like a rope (the tendon) passing over a pulley (the foramen triosseum). The pectoralis muscle is responsible for the downstroke.

■   From what you know about the power stroke in flapping flight, which muscle is likely to be the larger, the supracoracoideus or the pectoralis?

In most birds the downstroke of the wing is the power stroke (Section 5.3) so you would expect the pectoralis muscle to be larger and indeed this is generally the case. For example, in the herring gull (*Larus argentatus*) the supracoracoideus muscle is very much smaller than the pectoralis, and if you get the opportunity to look at a domestic chicken you will find similarly that the pectoralis muscle is larger.

The contraction of both of the supracoracoideus muscles to produce an upstroke generates a force on the joint between the humerus and coracoid bones. If you look at Figure 5.16 and imagine the muscles contracting you can see that they will tend to pull the joint in towards the mid-line. Between the two joints is a U-shaped bone, the furcula, which is probably more familiar to you as the wishbone. It appears that this bone and its joint can store energy, like a spring, and perhaps act to provide an opposing force to the inward force generated when the supracoracoideus muscles contract. Information about the role of the furcula comes from cineradiographic analysis of starlings in flight. Traces from the film made in this study are shown in Figure 5.17. During the downstroke the furcula (Figure 5.18) bends laterally, springing back during the upstroke.

During the wingbeat cycle, the sternum also moves as the muscles attached to it contract. On the downstroke, the sternum moves upwards and backwards, dropping again and moving forward during the upstroke. A consequence of these bone movements is that the rib cage changes shape, altering the size of the thoracic cavity. So, there is a link between the wingbeat cycle and the respiratory cycle, though the scale of the contribution made by the flight muscle contractions to respiration is not yet known.

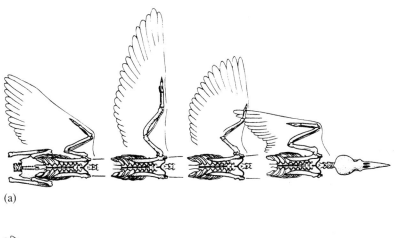

(a)

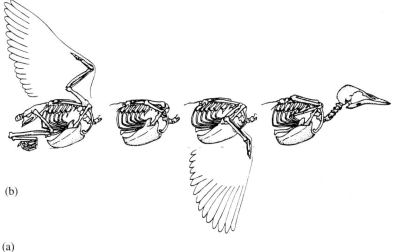

(b)

(a)

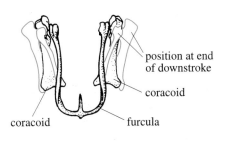

position at end
of downstroke

coracoid

coracoid   furcula

(b)

Figure 5.17   Analysis of the wingbeat cycle of a European starling (*Sturnus vulgaris*). (a) Dorsal and (b) lateral views of the bird in flight.

Figure 5.18   The furcula and the coracoids of the starling. These bones bend laterally during flight.

Summary of Section 5.6

The downstroke of the wing is the power stroke in most species of bird and in these species the pectoralis muscle, which produces the downstroke, is substantially larger than the supracoracoideus, which produces the upstroke. Both muscles lie below the point of articulation of the wing. The supracoracoideus has a long tendon which is attached to the dorsal surface of the humerus so that although the muscle lies below the point of articulation, the force it develops is transmitted via the tendon to the upper surface of the humerus, so raising the wing.

5.7 The wake

In Section 2.3.2 you read about the studies of locomotion in fluids that have concentrated on the wake left by fish moving through the water. There have also been a number of studies of the wake of birds, though as the wake is such a short-lived phenomenon, and normally invisible, such studies have not been easy. Nikolai Kokshaysky worked on this problem at the Severtzov Institute in Moscow in the late 1970s using chaffinches that he had trained to fly between two perches positioned a few metres apart. As a bird flew between the perches, he blew wood dust into the air. The dust took up the shape of the bird's wake. To photograph the wake, he carried out the experiments in darkness and used an infrared beam to detect the flight of the bird and trigger a series of flash guns. Two cameras at right angles to each other recorded the wake pattern. Some of Kokshaysky's photographs are shown in Figure 5.19.

Figure 5.19d shows a vortex ring formed behind the bird. This was not the first time that such vortices had been observed, but these are the first photographs to show vortex formation in birds.

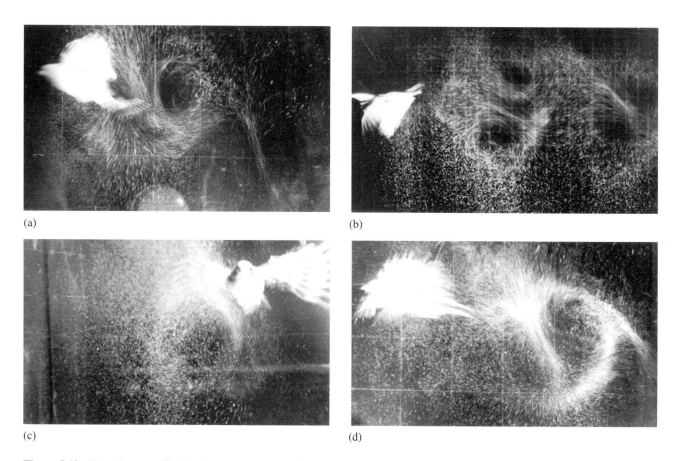

(a)

(b)

(c)

(d)

Figure 5.19   Four photographs taken by Nikolai Kokshaysky of a chaffinch flying through an atmosphere of wood dust in a darkened room. The flashes were triggered as the bird flew through an infrared beam. (a) The effect of a single downstroke. (b) The wake resulting from a series of three downstrokes. The wake seen from the front (c) and simultaneously from the side (d). A vortex ring is visible in the wake of the bird in photograph (d).

The air movements that produce such effects were observed a long time ago in aircraft, but the significance was not immediately apparent. Here is an account of such observations, written many years after the event.

> The author has vivid memories of an incident when, on a festive occasion, long streamers were attached to the wing-tips of his flying boat. When taxying on the water, these streamers rotated violently and they continued to do so in the air until, after a few minutes, they were nothing but shreds. The author and his colleagues dismissed the whole affair with such silly remarks as "That was funny, wasn't it?" Had they been a little more intelligent they would have realized that a phenomenon of this kind does not occur without good reason and they would have followed it up by further experiment – and maybe it would have slowly dawned on them that this was one of the most significant facts of aviation and one that was to influence the whole trend of aeroplane design. But that discovery was left to others and, even then, it took a long time.
>
> A. C. Kermode (1930)

What Kermode had observed was the consequence of the air flow being in a spiral form as it left the trailing edge of the wing of his aircraft. You can reproduce the observation by attaching thin, lightweight streamers to the tips of the wings of a balsawood glider and launching it into the air. The streamers should take up a spiral form, rotating clockwise on one side and anti-clockwise on the other. It may not be easy to see this! Alternatively, hold the glider in the air stream from a hairdryer and you should see the streamers spiral backwards from the wing.

Figure 5.20 shows the airflow over a fixed wing. As the air flows off the trailing edge of the wing it is deflected downwards and inwards, imparting a clockwise rotation to the airflow from the right-hand wing and an anti-clockwise one from the left-hand one. The wake that is formed is a continuous pair of spirals. How, then, is a vortex formed in birds?

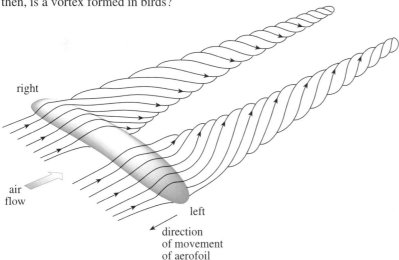

Figure 5.20 The wake created by a fixed aerofoil as it moves through the air. Note that the direction of the spiral is inwards on each side, imparting a clockwise rotation (seen from the front) on the right of the aerofoil and an anti-clockwise one on the left.

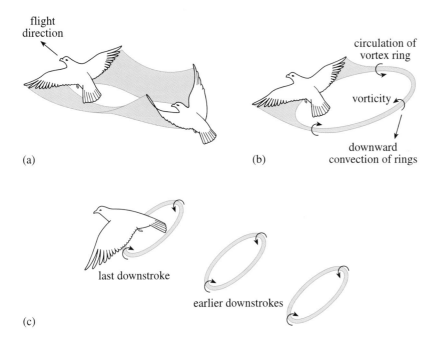

(a)

(b)

circulation of
vortex ring

vorticity

downward
convection of rings

(c)

last downstroke

earlier downstrokes

Figure 5.21   The generation of a vortex ring in flight. (a) The vortex sheet shed during the first part of the downstroke of the wing. (b) The vortex ring half formed. (c) The complete vortex ring is shed at the end of the downstroke – two previous vortices, the products of the previous two wingbeat cycles, are also shown.

In flapping flight, as Figure 5.19 shows, a vortex is formed on the downstroke of the wing. Figure 5.21a shows how, as the wings move down, two vortex sheets form, one from each wing. The sheets roll up to form a half-ring (Figure 5.21b) and then, as the downstroke is completed, the vortex is shed as a complete ring (Figure 5.21c). The wings are flexed during the upstroke, have little interaction with the air and produce little vorticity: recall that it is the downstroke that normally generates the power (Section 5.3).

The significance of the vortex for the physiologist is that because it represents the reaction of the air to the bird moving through it, observations and measurements of the vortices produced by birds can yield valuable information about aerodynamic forces, mechanical energetics, wing design and other features of flight. For example, Figure 5.22 shows that each vortex ring is tilted from the horizontal. The angle of tilt is related to the thrust-to-weight ratio of the bird. Jeremy Rayner, at Bristol University, has been in the forefront of this work. Indeed, he published a theoretical model of vortex formation in the same year that Nikolai Kokshaysky published his photographs of the chaffinch. Subsequently, Jeremy Rayner worked with bubbles to photograph the wake left by a number of species of birds and, with Gareth Jones at Bristol, the wake left by bats. He filled soap bubbles with a mixture of helium and air, such that they were neutrally buoyant. As the animal flew through the cloud of bubbles, a linear series of flashguns was triggered in sequence. A pair of cameras took stereo images which showed the moving bubbles as a series of dots, the distance between each position of a bubble on the film representing the time between two flashes and the distance that the bubble had travelled in that time.

A flying bird must expend energy to generate the vortices, and this is equivalent to the energy necessary to overcome induced drag. So, one might imagine that there would be an advantage in not producing vortices since a component of drag would be absent. However, this is not the case. The only way in which

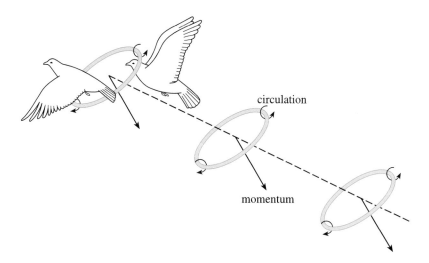

Figure 5.22 The chain of vortex rings that forms in the wake of a bird in forward flight.

forward movement can be imparted to the bird by flapping flight is if there is a transport of momentum to the air. The direction and speed of movement of the vortex ring backwards is indicative of the magnitude and direction of the force that created it. So, for optimum flight conditions, the wake generated should provide the maximum momentum transport for the minimum energy input. Experiments and theory both suggest that there are only a few types of wake that are associated with efficient flight. The optimum structures are rings, loops or spirals. Figure 5.23 shows the wake produced by a falcon (*Falco* sp.) in cruising flight, where the wing produces some lift on the upstroke. The wake is very like that produced by an aircraft and, when the bird is gliding, the wake is a pair of linear vortices, the continuous vortex wake, as you would have seen in the balsawood glider experiment mentioned earlier.

Figure 5.23 The continuous vortex wake of a falcon.

The type of wake can be related to the lifestyle of the animal. In all species so far studied, a vortex ring wake is produced during slow flight and, where the wings are broader and more rounded, in fast and cruising flight. Animals with longer, thinner wings, such as falcons, kestrels, swallows, swifts and pipistrelle bats, change to a continuous vortex as speed increases. They may maintain this type of wake when subsequently decelerating. The types of wake are analogous with the gaits that are described for terrestrial animals. Only the two types of gait described above have been observed so far and it is unlikely that any more exist, apart perhaps from some very specialized cases.

5.8 Conclusion

Aerodynamic theory derived from the development of aviation has provided a theoretical framework for the study of flight in birds. The primary difference between an aircraft and a bird, in terms of the aerodynamic forces acting on them, is that the wings of an aircraft provide lift and it derives its thrust from an engine, whereas in a bird the wings provide both lift and forward movement. Birds evolved from reptiles, but as the ability to fly evolved the skeleton became lighter, the forelimbs became substantially modified, the scales were replaced by feathers and the muscles involved in forelimb movement changed substantially. The shape of the wings in a particular species is an adaptation to a particular mode of life such as soaring, gliding or fast flapping flight. A measure of the shape of a wing is the aspect ratio, the ratio of the wing span to the mean chord.

Birds in flight are subject to a drag force that has a number of components. One of these, induced drag, is a consequence of the formation of a wake. The wakes of birds flying under laboratory conditions have been visualized using wood particles or bubbles containing helium. The wake has revealed the formation of vortices in either rings or linear spirals. These two types of wake are called gaits, in a similar way to the locomotory patterns of terrestrial animals. The study of gaits has provided information about the aerodynamics of flight.

Studying the dynamics of bird flight throws up important energetic considerations—how do you estimate the costs of flight or, more importantly, measure them under realistic conditions? Wake visualization, together with vortex theory, has provided a means of estimating mechanical energy consumption in flight, but it is the coupling of aerodynamic theory and observation with the measurement of physiological parameters, such as heart rate in free-flying birds, that has provided the real advance in our understanding of the energetics of flight. It is the energetic cost of flying and the occurrence of flying in other groups of animals that we consider in the next chapter.

Objectives for Chapter 5

After completing Chapter 5 you should be able to:

5.1   Define and use, or recognize definitions and applications of, each of the **bold** terms.

5.2   Explain how an aerofoil moving through air generates lift.

5.3   Draw a diagram illustrating the forces acting on a bird in flight and describe the forces in non-mathematical terms.

5.4   Draw outline diagrams of, or label diagrams of, the shape of typical, identified, birds and explain how they are adapted to their particular flight strategy.

5.5   Use diagrams to explain how the musculature of a bird produces the flapping flight movements of the wing and how the wing generates both lift and thrust.

5.6   Describe techniques used for visualizing air flow in experiments with flying birds and explain the physiological significance of the results from such experiments.

5.7   Describe the two typical gaits observed in flying animals and relate them to particular types of flight.

Questions for Chapter 5

(Answers to questions are at the end of the book.)

Question 5.1 (Objectives 5.1, 5.2 and 5.3)

For each of the following statements about flight, decide whether the statement is true or false and explain why.

(a)   Aspect ratio describes the cross-sectional area of a wing.

(b)   A bird flying slowly would reduce the angle of incidence of its wings to increase lift.

(c)   Induced drag and profile drag arise from the active flapping of the wings in birds.

Question 5.2 (Objective 5.4)

Look at the drawings of the two bird wings, in Figure 5.24a and b. For each describe the aspect ratio of the wing and the probable style of flight of the owner.

(a)

(b)

Figure 5.24   Wing shapes of two birds (not drawn to scale). For use with Question 5.2.

Question 5.3 (Objective 5.5)

In a few brief statements, describe the muscular events that occur, in sequence, from the bottom of one downstroke of a bird's wing until the bottom of the next. Indicate the direction of the forces involved and the bones that the muscles act upon.

Question 5.4 (Objective 5.6)

Outline one technique that has been used to visualize the wake of a flying bird. What is the value, to physiologists, of the pictures of the wake that can be obtained.

Question 5.5 (Objective 5.7)

What are the two gaits observed in birds? Under what conditions can a bird change from one gait to another?

Plate 5.1 The gannet (*Sula bassana*) gliding near the Bass Rock.

(a)

(b)

(c)

(d)

(e)

(f)

Plate 6.1 Gliding vertebrates: (a) the Javan flying frog (*Rhacophorus reinwardti*, length 8 cm); (b) the flying fish (*Exocoetus volitans*, length 20 cm); (c) the flying lizard or dragon (*Draco volans*, length 20 cm); (d) Kuhl's gecko (*Ptychozoon kuhli*, length 15 cm); (e) the paradise tree snake (*Chrysopelea* sp., length 1.5 m); (f) the Southern flying squirrel (*Glaucomys volans*, length 25cm).

and the efficiency of conversion of metabolic energy into mechanical energy. These measurements are complex but, as Jeremy Rayner has written:

> It is the quantification of these factors, as they apply to the life history of an individual animal, which is the greatest challenge in the study of flight.

6.2 Gliding and parachuting

Non-powered flight is loosely termed gliding, but a distinction is often made between gliding and parachuting. In gliding, the angle between the horizontal and the glide path is less than 45°, whereas in parachuting the angle is greater than 45°. This is illustrated in Figure 6.1 for a flying squirrel (a) and a parachuting frog (b).

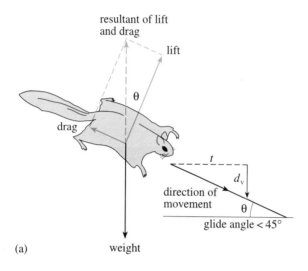

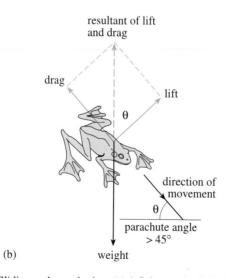

Figure 6.1   Gliding and parachuting. (a) A flying squirrel gliding at an angle of less than 45°. The sinking speed is equal to the vertical distance moved divided by the time taken (d_v/t). (b) A frog parachuting to the ground at an angle greater than 45°. The area of the 'aerofoil' supporting the weight is larger in a gliding animal than in a parachuting one.

6.2.1 Frogs

Some species of frog are able to glide and their glide angles can be surprisingly shallow. An Australian frog (*Hyla miliaria*) has been observed to descend at an angle of only 18°. When a frog jumps into the air at the start of a flight the legs are outstretched, with the hindlegs being moved round into the gliding position after take-off. The webs between the digits are larger on the rear legs and they provide the majority of the lift. The front legs, with their smaller surface area, act as stabilizers. With the legs in the gliding position the lift is behind the centre of gravity. In general, species of gliding frog have been found to have quite shallow glide angles, around 30°, which suggests that the combination of low wing loading together with the other adaptations is particularly efficient.

It is not clear why frogs glide or parachute. There are a number of arboreal species that have well-developed webs between the digits on their limbs, for example *Rhacophorus reinwardti* and *Agalychnis spurrelli* (Plates 6.1a and 6.3, respectively), which suggests that there are advantages in gliding. The most likely selection pressure on such frogs is predation, but for arboreal frogs the ability to glide between branches of trees may confer advantages in the search for food and water. However, in one species, studied in the early part of the twentieth century, the stomach contents of some specimens were found to include remains of insects which were only active at night and were not found on the trees. It remains a possibility, however, that for some species, gliding is partly an adaptation to feeding.

In addition to the species that glide, there are others that can reduce their rate of descent in air, but cannot achieve a shallow glide angle—they can only parachute.

6.2.2 Fish

Marine fish

Flying fish are one of the memorable sights for ocean travellers in the tropics. The fish leap out of the water and glide over the surface, apparently for quite long distances. Flying fish occur throughout the tropics and there are several species of such fish in one family—the Exocoetidae. The best known is *Exocoetus*, a fish of about 20 cm overall length. *Exocoetus volitans* is shown in Plate 6.1b. The pectoral fins, which are situated close to the centre of gravity, are greatly enlarged, forming wings. The body is thin and the lower lobe of the tail or caudal fin is enlarged. A second form of flying fish is exemplified by the genus *Cypselurus*, where both the pectoral and pelvic fins are enlarged to form wings and the lower lobe of the caudal fin is also enlarged (Figure 6.2). The two types of fish are referred to as the monoplane (single wings) and biplane (paired wings) types, respectively. There are aerodynamic differences between them. The monoplane arrangement of wings maximizes speed while the biplane arrangement maximizes lift. The biplane species have lower aspect ratio wings and a lower wing loading for equivalent body mass, giving increased lift at lower speeds (Chapter 5).

Figure 6.2   The flying fish *Cypselurus*, showing the enlarged pectoral and pelvic fins that form the wings and the asymmetrical tail, or caudal fin.

When a fish leaps through the water surface into the air it can glide, but it is not capable of powered flight. Thus, it will descend as the drag of the air over the body reduces its forward velocity. A long gliding distance can only be achieved if the initial velocity is high. For example, with an exit velocity of $25 \, \mathrm{m \, s^{-1}}$, the gliding distance is around 50 m at a maximum of 6 m or so above the water.

The flying fish can increase the distance travelled by powerful movements of its tail as it starts to sink back into the water. The enlarged lower lobe of the caudal fin can generate sufficient power when immersed to provide additional lift and thrust that will propel the fish forward through the air again. By repeating this tail movement, the fish can travel several hundred metres before returning to the water.

When taking-off, the genus *Cypselurus* taxis with the elongated lower lobe of the caudal fin in contact with the water, generating thrust which increases the take-off speed from $10 \, \mathrm{m \, s^{-1}}$ to $16\text{–}20 \, \mathrm{m \, s^{-1}}$. Once the body of the fish is clear of the water the pectoral fins open with a small positive angle of incidence, generating lift. The pelvic fins then open, lifting the tail out of the water. The average length of the taxi before take-off is 9 m.

The selective advantage that flying gives to fish is thought to be the ability to escape from predators. So, flight might originally have developed as an escape mechanism and has subsequently become the normal mode of locomotion for the fish because if they are able to maximize the time out of water, they minimize the risk from predation. This theory is an attractive one, but there is no evidence for it and there is one problem that it does not address. The selection pressure acting on the fish would be unlikely to produce much selective advantage until the adaptations were well developed and the fish could fly. If the selection pressure of predation is so strong, it is odd that so few fish species have adaptations that permit flight. Many species leap out of the water when escaping predators and it is not clear that flying is necessarily a better strategy than jumping, which does not require any special adaptations, beyond high power output.

An alternative explanation for the evolution of flying in fish comes from the energy costs of locomotion. Jeremy Rayner has suggested that as the drag experienced by the fish moving through water is some 800 times greater than it would be in air, a fish that could glide in air would have a reduced cost of locomotion per metre travelled. The saving in energy costs would be significant since energy to overcome drag would be stored as kinetic and potential energy, rather than being used to counteract drag during sustained swimming. It is interesting to note that the species of fish that fly, feed on plankton near the surface, where the drag is greater than in deep water.

One group of fish that was once believed to be able to fly is that of the flying gurnards – the Dactylopteridae. *Dactylopterus volitans*, which is found in the tropical Atlantic and the Red Sea, is shown in Plate 6.4. The ancient Greeks and Romans commented on how spectacular their flight was and described them as 'swallows'. However, in recent studies they have not been observed to fly and it is likely that they have been confused with other species of flying fish.

Freshwater fish

There are two families of freshwater fish that contain species that fly. The hatchet fish are the only fish that use flapping flight. These small fish flap their pectoral fins in the air and can travel up to 5 m in air, 500 body lengths. The musculature around the pectoral fins is extensive and is used to move the fins under water to provide propulsion and directional control. The action of the muscles in air is an extension of their role underwater. The fish feed on insects above the surface, while they are flying.

■ What physiological, rather than aerodynamic, limit might there be on the total flying distance?

Although hatchet fish do use flapping flight, it is very unlikely that each flight could be very long. The supply of oxygen to the flight muscles effectively ceases in air as the gills cannot take up oxygen. So, the limit to flight will almost certainly be oxygen supply, and it is likely that there are periods of rest between flights to allow for the uptake of recovery oxygen from the water.

6.2.3 Lizards and snakes

The tropical forests of southeast Asia are the home of the flying lizard *Draco volans* (Plate 6.1c). This small lizard of the agamid family is particularly well-adapted for gliding. Seven ribs on each side of the body are elongated and they support a thin membrane, called the patagium, which acts as an aerofoil. The animal can alter the angle of incidence of the patagium to the airflow, which adjusts the rate of descent. The long tail provides a substantial measure of control and lizards have been seen to glide through very small gaps between trees with ease. The flight pattern of these lizards has been studied and filmed. Take-off is simply a jump into the air from a tree. The lizard descends steeply at first, building up kinetic energy, but then raises the leading edge of the patagium.

■   What effect would raising the leading edge of the patagium have?

Raising the leading edge would increase the airflow over the patagium, so generating lift, slowing the rate of descent and increasing the distance the lizard could glide. Indeed, the final glide angle can be as little as 15°.

■   The angle of incidence of the patagium is changed just before landing. Would you expect the angle of incidence to decrease or increase?

The angle of incidence of the patagium would increase just before landing, which puts the patagium into the equivalent of a stall. Lift would disappear and the lizard would land easily.

There are around twenty species of *Draco* and all occupy a similar niche in the rainforest. They feed on ants, and their ability to fly enables them to move around in the forest with little expenditure of energy. Moreover, feeding normally occurs while the animal is climbing up a tree, and it seems that feeding while climbing down one is difficult. The ability to drop rapidly to the bottom of the same tree or a neighbouring one and then ascend the trunk again may well be a feeding adaptation.

Other lizards with adaptations to flight are known, such as the gecko *Ptychozoon* (Plates 6.1d and 6.5), but their glide angle is steep and they should be regarded as parachutists rather than gliders. A remarkable parachuting reptile is found in the jungles of Borneo and it is an example of an unlikely traveller's tale being found to be true. The paradise tree snake *Chrysopelea* (Plate 6.1e), has been shown to be capable of parachuting and possibly gliding. Film of this snake, taken by the BBC Natural History Unit, shows the snake projecting itself from a high tree branch and then gliding towards the ground. The body of the snake is thrown into a coil (Figure 6.3) and then held rigid while the tail controls the glide. The skin on the ventral surface of the body is drawn inwards as the ribs are flexed, creating a concave surface that faces the airflow as the body coil is held in the horizontal plane. In this respect, the body of the snake is acting like a parachute. However, to achieve a glide angle as shallow as less than 45° would probably require some additional aerodynamic feature that, at present, we can only speculate about. Gliding and parachuting in *Chrysopelea* is a truly remarkable sight and seems to defy our understanding of animal flight.

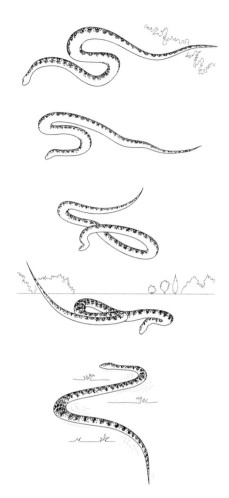

Figure 6.3   The flying snake *Chrysopelea* showing the shape of the body in flight (drawn from film).

6.2.4 Mammals

The most familiar flying mammals are the bats, which are capable of flapping flight. However, there are three orders of mammals that contain species which have adaptations to gliding: the Marsupialia, the Rodentia and the Dermoptera. These adaptations have appeared independently in the three orders, but all involve the development of a membrane that stretches between the forelimbs and hindlimbs (Figure 6.4). Some species have extensions to the membranes, connecting the hindlimbs to the tail and the forelimbs to the neck.

Interestingly, flight adaptations have even evolved independently *within* one order—the Marsupialia (Figures 6.4a and 6.6). There are three genera of marsupials that have membranes connecting the forelimbs and hindlimbs, but all three seem to have evolved separately. Of the rodents, fifteen closely-related genera from two families are adapted for gliding (Figure 6.4b). Finally, the colugo (Figure 6.4c) is unusual in that it is the only member of the order Dermoptera that can fly. The colugo is often called the 'flying lemur' though it is not closely related to the true lemurs, which are in a different order.

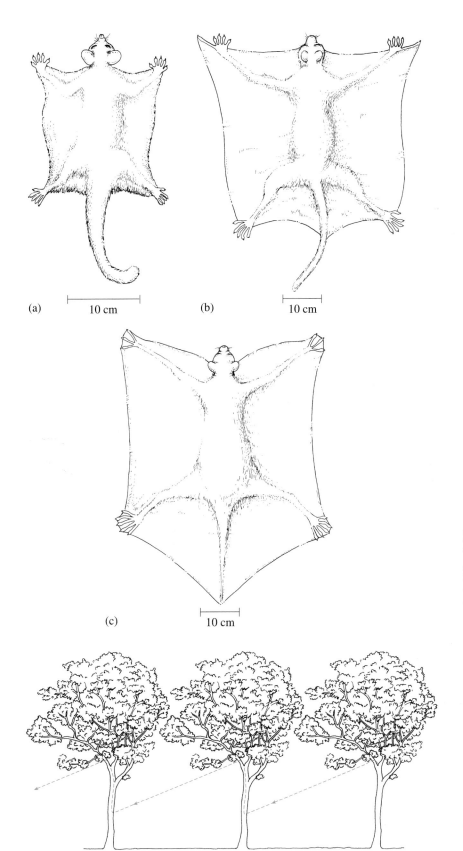

(a)   10 cm

(b)   10 cm

(c)   10 cm

Figure 6.4   Gliding mammals drawn to different scales. (a) The marsupial sugar glider *Petaurus breviceps*; (b) the giant flying squirrel *Petaurista petaurista*; (c) the Malayan colugo *Cynocephalus variegatus.*

Figure 6.5 The flight paths of flying squirrels through a forest.

Gliding has evolved at least seven times in mammals, but there are a number of features that all the different species have in common; they are all small (body mass up to 10 g) arboreal mammals that are largely vegetarian and nocturnal. It is the nocturnal habit that has ensured that they are a relatively little-known group of mammals.

One of the best studies of the gliding habit in mammals is that carried out in Borneo by Keith Scholey of the University of Bristol. He made observations of the flight of the largest of the flying squirrels *Petaurista petaurista* (Figure 6.4b). The squirrels emerged at dusk and he was able to observe them as they searched for fresh young leaves, gliding from one tree to another (Figure 6.5). He recorded the start and end positions of each glide, together with the time taken for the glide. When daylight came he could measure the distance travelled in each glide, and he found that the maximum distance was 130 m. The mean rate of descent was quite fast, with the squirrel losing height at the rate of $3\,\mathrm{m\,s^{-1}}$ when travelling with a ground speed of $15\,\mathrm{m\,s^{-1}}$. The wing loading (Section 5.2.1) is higher in a squirrel than a typical gliding bird, being nearly three times that of a buzzard.

■   What is the consequence for gliding speed of a high wing loading?

If the wing loading is high, the glide is fast, so that the air flow over the wing generates sufficient lift. The glide path of the squirrel is steep to start with and it loses height at a rate of $6\,\mathrm{m\,s^{-1}}$. As speed builds up, the glide then becomes shallower. The final ground speed is around $15\,\mathrm{m\,s^{-1}}$ (Figure 6.5).

■   Can you suggest how the squirrel might slow down and land safely?

You have read in Section 6.2.3 how the flying lizard *Draco volans* altered the angle of the patagium as it approached its landing point so that the patagium stalled and lift was lost. The flying squirrel does a similar thing by veering upwards and regaining some height just before landing. As it rears up, the 'wing' stalls and lift is lost. Obviously such a landing requires a great deal of control, but squirrels are adept at gliding and can even perform 180° turns in flight.

■   How might the squirrel exert control over its flight path?

As the membrane is attached to the limbs, it is possible for the squirrel to use the limbs to make small adjustments to the angle of attack of the membrane and hence change the amount and direction of lift. All the gliding rodents have a spine, made of cartilage, that supports the membrane. The spine is attached to the forelimbs, although the evolutionary origin of the spine and its position is different in the two families of rodents. In one, the spine is attached to the wrist, in the other to the elbow. A dramatic example of another species of flying squirrel, from the USA, is shown in Plate 6.1(f).

There are two questions of general interest that arise from looking at these gliding mammals:

1   Why has the adaptation to gliding arisen on several separate occasions in the mammals?

2   Are the gliding mammals a stage in the evolution of true flapping flight, as we see in the bats?

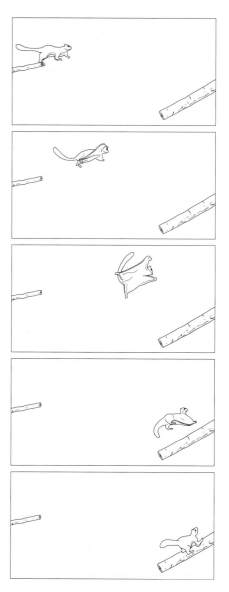

Figure 6.6   The marsupial sugar glider *Petaurus breviceps* in flight.

To provide an answer to the second question, we need to consider the adaptations to flight found in bats, which is the subject of the next section. The answer to the question of why gliding has evolved on several separate occasions lies in an investigation of the energetic costs of flight, which you will read about in Section 6.5.

Summary of Section 6.2

All five vertebrate classes have members that can fly, although powered flight is restricted to birds, bats and one species of freshwater fish, and only members of the first two groups are capable of sustained, powered flight. Amongst the reptiles and amphibians there is a range of adaptations to flying, all of which are concerned with increasing the surface area on which air can act. The distinction between gliding and parachuting is based on the angle of descent to the horizontal—the glide angle. If this is greater than 45°, the animal is normally considered to be parachuting and therefore to have less control. However, such a distinction is a rather arbitrary one.

The selective pressures that produced adaptations to flight vary amongst the species. In marine fish, flight may be a method of locomotion that has a reduced energetic cost per unit of distance covered. In freshwater fish, flight may be a feeding adaptation.

Flight has arisen independently in a number of groups of mammals. There is a surprising degree of convergence in the structure of the flight membranes.

6.3 Flight in bats

Bats are the only mammals capable of flapping flight. They are very diverse, with over 1 000 recognized species, and thus almost one-quarter of mammal species known are bats. They range in size from 2 g to 1 kg (adult body mass) and most feed on insects, although there are a number of tropical species that feed on fruit. There are also some more specialized bats that feed on nectar or pollen, fish, frogs or mammalian blood.

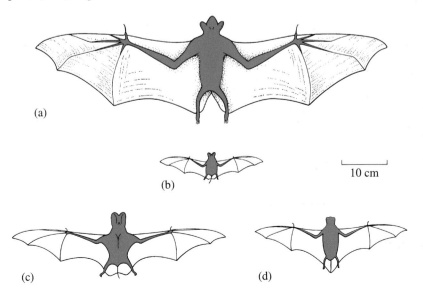

10 cm

Figure 6.7 The wing outlines of four species of bat, drawn to the same scale. (a) *Eidolon helvum* is a fruit-eating bat; (b) *Tadarida pumila*; (c) *Otomops martiensseni* and (d) *Nyctalus noctula* are insectivorous bats. *Tadarida* and *Nyctalus* are fast, high-flying species.

There are two families of bats—the Megachiroptera and the Microchiroptera. There is a debate among researchers on bats as to whether flight evolved separately in each of the two families, or just once in some ancestor common to them both.

The bat wing is a thin membrane stretched between the greatly elongated digits of the hand, the body and the hindlimbs. Unlike the bird wing, the skin that forms the wing membrane is bare with nothing that is equivalent to feathers. Some typical wing outlines of bat species are shown in Figure 6.7. A slow-flying bat, *Plecotus auritus*, is capable of hovering.

The structure of a bat wing is shown in Figure 6.8. The bone structure is a modified form of the mammalian forelimb structure. The movement in the wrist and elbow joints is restricted to the plane of the wing so that the wing does not twist in flight. The ulna bone is very small in comparison with the radius (Figure 6.9c)—this prevents the rotational movement that is possible in our own wrist joints. The wing membrane, of course, has to be kept under tension during flight or the air flow over it would not be laminar and lift would be reduced. Figure 6.8 shows how the forces of tension (blue arrows) and compression (grey arrows) in the wing keep it taut. There is a muscle in the forearm that inserts onto the second digit, pulling it forward and away from the third digit (shown by the long, thin black arrow). The force exerted by this muscle, the extensor carpi radialis longus, keeps the third digit extended, as the force the muscle exerts on the second digit is transmitted to the third by a ligament. The hindlimb pulls towards the body, which exerts a force on the membrane in opposition to that pulling the second and third digits forward, maintaining tension in the wing.

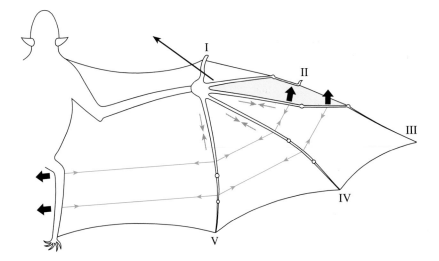

Figure 6.8   The right wing of a bat, spread as in flight. The blue arrows show the forces of tension in the membrane and the grey arrows the forces of compression in the bones. The thick black arrows show the direction in which the forearm muscle and the hindlimbs exert a force on the wing.

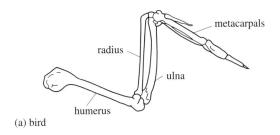

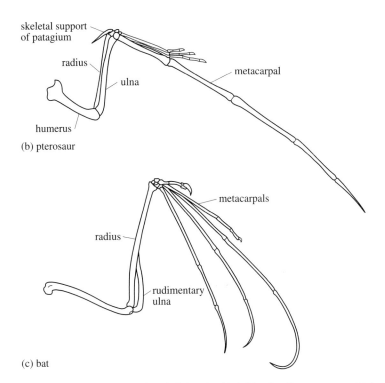

Figure 6.9 Modifications of the forelimb in (a) a bird (b) a fossil pterosaur and (c) a bat, showing the lengthening of the digits and the lightening of the bones. Note the almost complete loss of the ulna in bats.

In bats, the pectoralis muscle is the largest of the flight muscles but it is smaller, in relative terms, than the pectoralis in a bird (Section 5.6). The overall mass of the flight muscles in bats is less, in proportion to body weight, than in birds, being some 12% or so of body weight compared with 15–20% in birds (Section 6.4). In bats, the sternum to which the muscles are attached is larger than in rodents, but it does not reach the same proportions as the sternum in birds which is a much enlarged, keeled structure.

In flight, the downstroke is the powerstroke, as in the majority of birds (Section 5.6). During the upstroke, the wing membrane is slightly convex, indicating that lift is being generated. The wing can also present a negative angle of incidence to the airflow during the upstroke, which generates lift. The upstroke in birds rarely produces lift, hummingbirds and falcons being notable exceptions. Further aerodynamic differences between birds and bats are apparent from a comparison of both their aspect ratio and wing loading values (Figure 6.10).

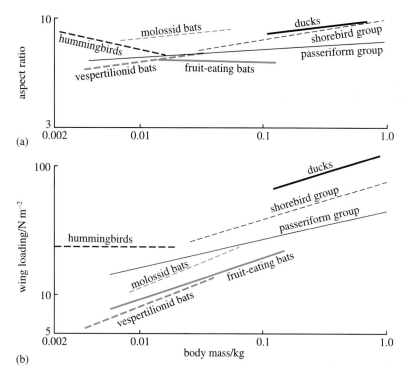

Figure 6.10   (a) Aspect ratio and (b) wing loading plotted against body mass in some groups of bats and birds. Note the log scales.

■   From Figure 6.10a and b what can you deduce about the aspect ratio and the wing loading of the bat wing, in comparison to that of birds?

Wing loading is generally lower in bats than in birds, and aspect ratio is also lower in two of the three groups of bats.

■   Is the fact that the aspect ratio is lower for a given body mass related to the wing loading?

A lower aspect ratio wing in a bat of the same body mass as a bird would mean that the bat had wings of a greater surface area and hence a smaller figure for wing loading. Generally, bats do not fly particularly fast in comparison with birds, but they have an impressive agility in the air. One of the features that distinguishes bat flight from that of birds is the ability of bats to perform stall turns.

You read in Section 5.7 about the study of the wake of bats carried out by Gareth Jones and Jeremy Rayner. The types of wake left by bats show that bats divide into the two types of gait that are observed in birds.

■   Recalling your knowledge of gaits in birds, what gaits would you predict for the following bats: (a) *Plecotus auritus*, a broad-winged, slow-flying bat; and (b) *Nyctalus noctula*, a narrower-winged, fast-flying bat?

Both bats produce vortex rings during slow flight—the vortex ring gait—but *Nyctalus* switches to the continuous vortex gait as speed increases. This is similar to the picture in birds, where those with longer, thinner wings switch to the continuous vortex gait at speed.

Summary of Section 6.3

There are a number of similarities between bird and bats, but there are significant differences in wing design, and the upstroke in bats always produces lift. The shape of the wing makes bats more manoeuvrable than birds but their maximum flight speed is slower. The wings of bats generally have a lower aspect ratio and wing loading than have birds of the same body mass.

6.4 Flight muscles

The principal muscles that provide the power for flight are the pectoralis muscles and the supracoracoideus muscles (Section 5.6). In fast, flapping flight it is the pectoralis muscles that do most of the work. In terms of mass, the pectoralis muscles are, on average, 15–20% of body mass, but the supracoracoideus muscles are much smaller, being only 10–15% of the mass of the pectoralis muscles.

■   In some birds the difference in size between the two muscles is much less, with the supracoracoideus being larger, around 50% of the mass of the pectoralis muscle. Can you suggest what habits such a bird might have?

Birds that hover generate power on both the downstroke and the upstroke, with both strokes developing sufficient lift to support the body weight in hummingbirds. The supracoracoideus muscle is also large in penguins, which is related to their ability to swim under water.

The flight muscle of birds contains a variety of fibre types, as in fishes (Section 2.2) and mammals. Both red and white fibres are present, but the proportions differ between species, with the differences being generally related to lifestyle. The domestic chicken rarely flies any great distance and this fact correlates well with the proportions of the fibres found in the pectoralis muscle.

■   Which do you think is the predominant fibre in the pectoralis muscle of chicken?

Chicken breast meat is white, with white, fast glycolytic muscle fibres comprising some 67% of the total. Eleven per cent of the fibres are red, with the remaining 22% being intermediate. In contrast, in the hummingbird *Archilochus* the muscles are composed entirely of red fibres.

■   From what you know about the lifestyle of the pigeon, how would the fibre composition of the pectoralis muscle compare with that of the chicken?

Pigeons are capable of long periods of sustained flight. White muscle fibres are anaerobic and not adapted for sustained power output (Section 2.2). So, pigeons have pectoralis muscles that are rich in red fibres, comprising 86% of the total, enabling them to fly continuously for very long periods. In the vast majority of birds, the flight muscles contain predominantly red oxidative fibres.

The flight muscles are obviously major sites of metabolic activity and require substantial amounts of oxygen to be delivered to them. The heart is larger in a bird than in a mammal of the same size, though generally the heart rate is lower.

However, the heart rate of a hummingbird can reach 1 000 beats per minute. Figures for oxygen consumption and cardiac output are difficult to obtain, but measurements have been made on birds in wind tunnels and on birds flying freely with telemetry devices attached and these have given us a picture of the metabolic needs of a flying bird.

The oxygen consumption of a budgerigar can reach $55\,cm^3\,g^{-1}\,h^{-1}$. To compare this rate with that of a mammal of the same weight, a 50 g kangaroo rat (*Dipodomys*) uses up to $14\,cm^3\,g^{-1}\,h^{-1}$ when running at top speed. Such a high rate of oxygen usage by the bird is possible because the respiratory system is adapted to a faster rate of gas exchange. However, we might expect the cardiovascular system to be more efficient also. The density of blood cells in the blood (the haematocrit) of birds, and hence the carrying capacity of the blood, is much greater than that of reptiles and is little different from that of mammals. For a house sparrow at sea level the capacity of the blood is about 19 vol%, compared with 18 vol% for a small mammal. The haematocrit is 48%, compared with 45% for the mammal. Differences are observed between species of birds. For example, the haemoglobin of the duck has a lower affinity for O_2 than has that of the barnacle goose, which flies at high altitude. But the haematocrit of the duck is elevated under conditions of hypoxia, a change that is not observed in the barnacle goose.

The cardiac output of a budgerigar in flight has been estimated at 3.7 litres $kg^{-1}\,min^{-1}$, which is more than seven times the maximum that a human could sustain. This high output does not come entirely from an increase in heart rate but seems to be primarily due to an increase in the stroke volume of the heart (that is, the volume of blood pumped by the heart during one cycle of contraction). Interestingly, while the heart rate in bats is high, compared with birds, the cardiac output is lower. The stroke volume in proportion to heart mass is intermediate between that of a bird and that of a small land mammal. However, the haematocrit is higher, which enables more oxygen to be transported per unit volume of blood.

6.5 Flight energetics

In this chapter and the previous one, we have explored the different flight strategies adopted by vertebrates. The energetic costs of each of these strategies can be measured to provide a figure for the cost of transport. Predictably, there are some strategies that appear more expensive than others. Gliding and soaring are obviously energetically less expensive than flapping flight, but the advantages of flapping flight under some circumstances are such that the expenditure of large amounts of energy is beneficial.

Measuring the power output of flying birds is difficult, as was suggested in Section 5.7. Work by Vance Tucker at Duke University provides a good example of the difficulties of direct measurement. In order to compare the energetic costs of different types of flight in budgerigars, he trained each of his birds to fly in a wind tunnel while wearing a mask that was connected to an oxygen analyzer. At rest, the birds consumed $20\,W\,kg^{-1}$ of energy but when flying at $10\,m\,s^{-1}$, this figure rose to $120\,W\,kg^{-1}$. The difference between the two figures is the energetic cost of flight.

The power used by a budgerigar in flight is shown in Figure 6.11. The blue curve shows the power used in ascending flight at different flight velocities, while the grey curve shows descending flight. The middle, black curve shows the energy consumption during level bounding flight and it is apparent that bounding flight is only marginally more energetically expensive than descending flight. How does bounding flight differ from continuous flight?

6.5.1 Bounding flight

Bounding flight has been observed in a large number of bird species. The bird does not flap its wings all the time, but folds them in to the side of the body for a short interval between successive bouts of wing flapping. For example, the flight pattern of the siskin (*Carduelis spinus*) consists of flapping flight lasting about 0.25 s, during which the wings beat for about five complete cycles, followed by a period of 0.35 s when the wings are folded against the sides of the body. By folding the wings, drag is reduced.

■ Using your knowledge from Section 5.3, what components of drag would be reduced if the wings were folded?

Induced drag and profile drag would be reduced. The extra power required during the periods of flapping flight is less than that saved during the periods when the wings are folded, and the induced and profile components of drag are substantially smaller.

■ Would you expect bounding flight to save more energy at low flight speeds or at high ones?

Recall from Figure 5.7 that profile drag increases substantially as flight speed increases, which suggests that bounding flight ought to be advantageous only at high speeds and that at low speeds birds ought to beat their wings continuously. However, there are some birds that use bounding flight at slow speeds and some, such as the sunbird, even use bounding flight while hovering. So, the explanation for the observed behaviour in terms of profile drag is not complete.

Another factor involved in bounding flight may be the performance of the wing muscles. Generally, the metabolic energy required by muscles to do a particular amount of work is least when the muscles shorten at about one-third of their maximum rate. It is at this rate that muscles give their highest power output. Also, it is reasonable to postulate that the rate of contraction of the flight muscles during fast flight is the rate at which the muscles develop maximum power for minimum energetic cost. Evolution would tend to match the efficiency of the flight muscles to the movement of the wings. So, if a bird is flying below its maximum speed, it would be most efficient to use its wings intermittently and flap them fast rather than flap them more slowly but continuously, with the muscles contracting less efficiently.

Providing a bird has plenty of reserves of power, then bounding flight will mean that the muscles are producing twice the power output over half the time, but are doing it more efficiently and so making an overall saving in metabolic energy.

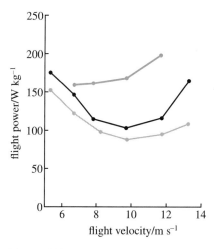

Figure 6.11 The power required for flight at different velocities for three different modes of flight in a budgerigar. The blue curve is ascending flight, the black curve is level, bounding flight and the grey curve is descending flight.

6.5.2 Flying in groups

By flying in groups, birds can make substantial savings in energy. It has been calculated that 25 birds flying in an extended line, wing tip to wing tip, could halve the power required for lift generation. This advantage comes about because the wing tip of each bird produces an updraft which reduces the lift required by the neighbouring bird. Of course, the birds at the ends of the line receive less benefit than those nearer the centre.

The classic 'V' formation seen in geese may have a further benefit. For example, the birds on the right-hand side of the 'V' fly with their left wing tip directly behind the right wing tip of the bird in front (Figure 6.12). The vortex trailing from the wing tip of the bird in front rotates in the opposite way to that produced by the wingtip of the next bird in the 'V'. As a consequence, the two air movements cancel each other out and no vortices are produced after the air has passed the second wingtip. Producing fewer vortices saves energy since the vortex represents kinetic energy transferred to the air.

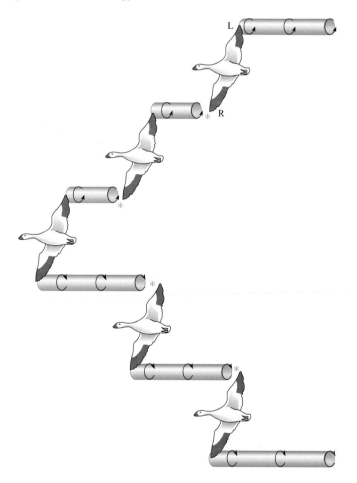

Figure 6.12   Geese flying in formation (viewed from below). Note that the left (L) and right (R) sides of the birds are marked on the top bird only. The vortex funnels from each wingtip are shown by the cylindrical shaded areas with arrows indicating the direction of air flow rotation. The blue asterisks indicate the points at which the vortices from the leading and following wingtips cancel each other out.

6.5.3 The cost of transport

In Section 5.3 you learned how the total flight power is related to the components of drag. Figure 6.13 is similar to Figure 5.7, but the data are taken from vortex measurements on a pigeon. The tangent to the curve for total power has been added (blue line). Taking the point where the tangent cuts the curve and projecting vertically downwards onto the *x*-axis, gives a figure for flight speed at which the cost of transport is a minimum. At any particular speed, the cost of transport (*C*) is given by

$$C = P/mgv$$

where *P* is the flight power output at a speed of *v* for a bird of mass *m* and *g* is the acceleration due to gravity. The cost of transport is the power required to carry unit weight of bird through unit distance.

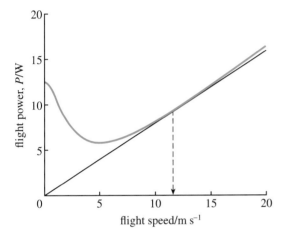

Figure 6.13 Flight power output against flight speed of a pigeon, measured using the vortex rings visualized behind the bird. The derivation of a value for the minimum cost of transport is shown by the vertical line between the tangent to the power curve and the *x*-axis.

By deriving a figure for flight power from Figure 6.13, for a 330 g bird flying at 5 m s^{-1}, the cost of transport is

$$C = 6/(0.33 \times 9.81 \times 5) = 0.37 \, \text{W kg}^{-1}\text{m}^{-1}$$

■ What are the costs of transport for the same bird at (a) 10 m s^{-1} and (b) 20 m s^{-1}?

The minimum cost of transport for this bird is 0.24 W kg^{-1} m^{-1} (at a flight speed of 11.7 m s^{-1}), which compares with 0.26 W kg^{-1}m^{-1} at 10 m s^{-1} and 0.25 W kg^{-1}m^{-1} at 20 m s^{-1}, so the cost does not vary much over quite a range of speeds.

Jeremy Rayner has calculated the cost of transport for a range of bird species and his data are shown in Figure 6.14 as the minimum cost of transport plotted against body mass.

■ What explanation can you offer for the fact that the larger and heavier birds have a lower minimum cost of transport?

The larger birds tend to have proportionally larger wings, which are necessary for take-off, but once flying the larger wings would make flight more efficient.

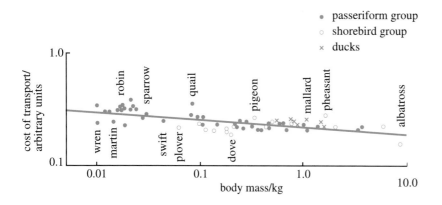

Figure 6.14   Theoretical calculations of the minimum cost of transport of 65 different species of bird, plotted against body mass. Note the log scales.

6.5.4 Energetic costs in gliding mammals

Gliding could have evolved in the mammals as a response to predation; gliding to another tree would be an obvious escape mechanism. However, there are energetic advantages to gliding in forests. It has been shown that compared with running, gliding allows an animal to move much faster and cover a greater distance. In the gliding squirrel *Petaurista*, studied by Keith Scholey (Section 6.2.4), the savings in energy that arise from the evolution of gliding enable the squirrel to forage over a much wider area. Gliding from tree to tree means that the squirrel does not have to descend to the ground to move to another tree in search of fruit, so there is a further saving in energy. It is, perhaps, these energetic advantages that have provided such a great selective advantage that gliding has arisen independently so many times in mammals. Gliding is probably also a stage in the evolution of bats. The fruit bats might well have taken the same evolutionary route as the gliding squirrels. If gliding has energetic advantages, then selection will favour those individuals that are more proficient at gliding. Increased 'wing' area or greater control during the glide will both confer increased fitness (the extent to which an organism is adapted to the surroundings) and it is easy to see that the range of adaptations to an aerial existence that we find in bats could have evolved from a gliding habit.

Summary of Section 6.5

There are a number of different flight strategies used by animals, and working out the energy requirements of flight is not easy. Bounding flight appears to be adopted primarily by small birds and to be a means of reducing the overall cost of flying. The wings flap for about half the time and for the rest of the time they are folded into the side of the body. Thus twice the power is needed from the wings for half the flight time, but there is an energy saving because the flight muscles are able to work at their optimum frequency of contraction.

The minimum cost of transport has been calculated from theoretical data for a large number of bird species and the overall picture is one of the larger, heavier birds having a slightly lower cost of transport.

Gliding has evolved independently several times in mammals and there are energetic advantages in the gliding habit for mammals that are arboreal. The bats have probably evolved from gliding ancestors.

6.6 Conclusion

Apart from the birds and bats, there are only a few species of vertebrate that can fly, but they do come from all five classes of vertebrate. Most of these other species glide or parachute and are not capable of powered flight. A distinction is made between gliding and parachuting on the basis of the angle at which the animal descends. If the angle between the descent path and the horizontal is always greater than 45°, then the animal is described as parachuting—simply slowing the rate of descent. At angles of less than 45°, the animal is gliding, and is obtaining some lift from extensions of the body or limbs.

Although there are many flying vertebrates, few of the individual species and groups have been well studied. Flight has evolved on many occasions in the vertebrates and there has been a surprising degree of convergence. This is partly because, from an aerodynamic point of view, the number of options is limited, but it might also be that flight has evolved through a gliding phase and the gliding phase has brought convergence. The obvious question is: are they a stage on the evolutionary path to powered flight, as exemplified by bats? An analysis of the energetic costs of species that glide suggests that there are advantages in gliding as there is a saving of energy. It might well be that the selective advantages gained by animals that could glide eventually led to the evolution of the bats from a gliding ancestor. Studies of flight of many of the gliding species have been limited because such animals are relatively inaccessible in forest areas. Birds and bats too present problems, for although many of them are much better known than gliding species, the fact that they are aerial makes them less easy to work with. It is the development of modern instrumentation and wind tunnels that has made work on birds and bats in flight possible. Modern electronics has made it possible for physiological instruments to be made so small that terrestrial animals can carry them around with a built-in radio transmitter. This technology can be used for flying animals too, but fitting a bird or bat with an instrument package that does not alter its aerodynamic characteristics, or so overload it that it cannot take off, is still a problem that has not been resolved. Few telemetric studies on free-flying animals have been carried out, but when they are, as they surely will be in the near future, we may get a much better understanding of the energy costs of flying.

Objectives for Chapter 6

After completing Chapter 6 you should be able to:

6.1 Define and use, or recognize definitions and applications of, each of the **bold** terms.

6.2 Distinguish between powered flight, gliding and parachuting and be able to quote examples that exemplify each method of locomotion.

6.3 Describe the adaptations to flight of flying fish, frogs and reptiles and state the aerodynamic significance of each adaptation.

6.4 List the similarities and differences in morphology between bats and birds and relate these to the flight styles of the animals.

6.5 Review the distribution of gliding in mammals and describe the mechanism in at least one named example.

6.6 Given suitable data, derive values for the cost of transport and the minimum flight speed in birds.

Questions for Chapter 6

(Answers to questions are at the end of the book.)

Question 6.1 (Objective 6.1)

What feature of the definition of the terms gliding flight and parachuting flight provides the key distinction between the two?

Question 6.2 (Objective 6.2)

Which of the following animals are gliders and which are parachutists?

(a)   *Chrysopelea*

(b)   *Draco volans*

(c)   *Petaurista petaurista*

(d)   *Exocoetus volitans*

(e)   *Hyla miliaria*

Question 6.3 (Objective 6.4)

From your knowledge of flight mechanisms in large birds, give two possible reasons why there are no bats of comparable size.

Question 6.4 (Objective 6.6)

Calculate the cost of transport for the following birds and then decide which is flying the most efficiently. Explain your answer.

Bird	Mass, m/kg	Flight speed, v/m s^{-1}	Power output, P/W	Cost of transport/W kg^{-1} m^{-1}
kestrel	0.20	8.1	1.8	
lapwing	0.21	9.1	2.7	
mallard	1.05	13.7	18.7	

EPILOGUE

This survey of animal performance has, of necessity, been a limited one. The range of measures that can be used to quantify performance, the variety of body plans and lifestyles found in animals, and the differences in the physical properties of the media in which animals move, all provide a rich diversity of subject matter. In concentrating on the details of just swimming and flight, this book has provided an interesting comparison between locomotion in two very different media. The examples chosen should have given you an insight into the rather specialized experimental techniques that are needed to study swimming and flying animals, and you will now appreciate that research into performance in free-living animals is driven as much by advances in technology as it is by advances in physiology.

Experimental techniques such as wake visualization have provided information on the energy requirements of flight, and it is instructive to compare these energetic costs with those of other forms of locomotion.

■ What measure could be used in a comparison of the costs of different forms of locomotion?

The most appropriate measure of energetic cost is the mass-specific metabolic rate. The rate of oxygen consumption of an animal can be converted into a rate of 'power input' or energy expenditure. Several factors influence the outlay of energy involved in moving a given mass of animal over a unit distance. One of these is inertia. The larger an animal, the greater is its inertia. However, the larger an animal, the greater is its momentum once it is moving. The drag experienced by an animal is influenced by both the surface area and the shape of the animal, together with the resistance to movement provided by the surrounding air or water. The cost of movement through water, which is more viscous and dense than air, is highly influenced by the larger drag forces, even on well-streamlined fish. In air, the drag forces have less significance, as air is less viscous. However, since the magnitude of the drag forces in air increases approximately as the square of the speed, streamlining is important for very fast birds. By contrast, terrestrial mammals are not usually streamlined because, for the speeds at which most mammals run, air resistance is slight.

Streamlining does not have the same significance for running. The metabolic cost of running decreases as body size, and hence mass, increases. However, for animals of approximately equivalent body mass, running is the most energetically expensive form of locomotion. During running, the centre of mass rises and falls cyclically. The muscles that push the body up and forward also have a role in braking the subsequent fall, and this requires further energy. Thus the efficiency of running is lower than that of other forms of locomotion, even if the contribution made by the storage of energy in elastic tendons (a factor which reduces the energetic costs of running) is ignored.

■ If you compared the energy costs of flying with the energy costs of swimming, which would be the more energetically expensive?

Although the drag forces are much higher in water than in air, swimming uses less energy than flying, so flying is the more energetically expensive form of locomotion.

■   Remembering that the drag forces in water are high, why do you think that the metabolic cost of swimming is low?

The energetic costs of overcoming the high drag forces in water are offset by the buoyancy of fish. The uplift provided by the water offsets, or even counterbalances, the effect of gravity, so little or no energy is expended in maintaining position. In contrast, birds in flight obtain little buoyancy from the air, and the output of the flight muscles has to generate both thrust and lift. However, a compensating fact is that birds are able to move at higher speeds than those usually attainable by runners of equivalent size, so the energetic costs of locomotion are not so high.

Hovering is much more expensive than flapping flight because there is little dynamic lift from the movement of the wings through the air. Some large birds economize by gliding, where the wings are not beating at all. This saves energy, because the flight muscles are active in an isometric rather than an isotonic state. The high efficiency of flapping flight is one of the reasons why birds can migrate over such vast distances in relatively short times.

The energetic costs of migration in birds are of great interest to the physiologist. Some birds are known to increase their food intake prior to migration, adding as much as 1.5 g of fat to their diet each day during the 10 days before departure. In the case of small species that migrate long distances, fat may make up 40% of the live weight of a bird. A generalized value for the energy required by a bird in migratory flight has been estimated to be $0.42 \, \text{kJ g}^{-1} \text{h}^{-1}$.

■   What facts would you need to know in order to calculate the maximum non-stop flight range of a bird?

Knowing the flight speed and the power-to-weight ratio (the ratio of the power produced by the muscles of a bird to the weight of that bird), we can calculate maximum ranges. Sample figures for small birds give distances of about 2 500 km, for shore birds 10 000 km and for humming birds 1 000 km. During migration, the ruby-throated humming bird flies a distance of about 900 km non-stop. This is close enough to the maximum range to leave little safety margin if weather conditions, such as wind direction, are unfavourable. We need data collected during actual flight to obtain a picture of how migrating birds utilise energy reserves and cope with adverse conditions.

What of the future? The miniaturisation of electronic components has enabled physiologists to attach telemetry devices to aquatic mammals, and to large bird species such as the albatross. The limiting factor in this type of study, apart from the expense and access to satellites, is the life of battery packs and their weight. As battery technology improves, so the size of animals capable of carrying long range transmitters will fall and the period over which data can be obtained will lengthen. The type of information that can be transmitted at present is generally insufficient for direct measurement of the metabolism of animals swimming or flying in their natural habitat, but indirect measures such as heart rate or breathing rate are already possible. The quest for an understanding of the total energy budget of an unstressed animal in its natural habitat is a key feature of physiological research.

GENERAL FURTHER READING

General

Alexander, R. McNeill (1992) *Exploring Biomechanics*, Scientific American Library, W. H. Freeman, New York. A beautifully illustrated account by the leading expert on biomechanics.

Bone, Q. and Marshall, N. B. (1982) *Biology of Fishes*, Chapman & Hall, New York. A good introduction to fish ecology, physiology and anatomy.

Day, M. H. (ed.) (1981) *Vertebrate Locomotion*, Symposia of the Zoological Society of London, No. 48, Academic Press, London. A collection of symposium papers covering the mechanics, physiology and energetics of flying, swimming and running.

Denny, M. W. (1993) *Air and Water*, Princeton University Press. A very good account of the biology and physics of life's media.

Duncan, G. (1990) *Physics in the Life Sciences* (2nd edition), Blackwell, Oxford. A physics book written for biologists. Contains experimental information and sections on fluids, temperature and heat.

Hill, R. W. (1976) *Comparative Physiology of Animals: An Environmental Approach*, Harper & Row, New York. An environmental approach to the physiology of swimming.

Hoar, W. S. and Randall, D. J. (1978) *Fish Physiology*, Academic Press, New York. A book that covers most aspects of fish physiology and includes chapters on swimming capacity, hydrodynamics, tuna physiology and fish muscle.

Kardong, K. V. (1995) *Vertebrates*, Wm. C. Brown Publishers, Iowa. A comparative account of the anatomy, evolution and function of vertebrates.

Kermode, A. C. (1930) *Flight without Formulae*, 5th edn (1989), Longman Group UK Ltd., Harlow. A well-written introduction to aerodynamics for pilots.

Rogers, E. (1985) *Looking at Vertebrates*, Longman. A practical book on vertebrates which includes photographs and drawings of skeletal structures.

Videler, J. J. (1993) *Fish Swimming*, Chapman & Hall, New York. An up-to-date, readable and well-illustrated account of all aspects of fish locomotion.

Specific subjects and original papers

Altringham, J. D. and Johnston, I. A. (1990) Modelling muscle power output in a swimming fish, *Journal of Experimental Biology*, **148**, 395–402.

Altringham, J. D., Wardle, C. S. and Smith, C. I. (1993) Myotomal muscle function at different locations in the body of a swimming fish, *Journal of Experimental Biology*, **182**, 191–206.

Block, B. A. and Booth, D. (1992) Direct measurement of swimming speeds and depth of blue marlin, *Journal of Experimental Biology*, **166**, 267–284.

Block, B. A., Finnerty, J. R., Stewart, A. F. R. and Kidd, J. (1993) Evolution of endothermy in fish: mapping physiological traits on a molecular phylogeny, *Science*, **260**, 210–214.

Dewar, H., Graham, J. B. and Brill, R. W. (1994) Studies of tropical tuna swimming performance in a large water tunnel, II Thermoregulation, *Journal of Experimental Biology*, **192**, 33–44.

Johnston, I. A. (1991) Muscle action during locomotion: a comparative perspective, *Journal of Experimental Biology*, **160**, 167–185.

Johnston, I. and Altringham, J. (1988) Muscle function in locomotion, *Nature*, **335**, 767–768.

Lucas, M. C., Priede, I. G., Armstrong, J. D., Gindy, A. N. Z. and Vera, L. de (1991) Direct measurements of metabolism, activity and feeding behaviour of pike, *Esox lucius* L., in the wild, by the use of heart rate telemetry, *Journal of Fish Biology*, **39**, 325–345.

Rayner, J.M.V. and Wooton, R.J. (1991) *Biomechanics in Evolution*, SEB Seminar Series No. 36, Cambridge University Press.

Rome, L. C., Swank, D. and Corda, D. (1993) How fish power swimming, *Science*, **261**, 340–342.

Rome, L. C., Funke, R. P., Alexander, R. McNeill, Lutz, G., Aldridge, H., Scott, F. and Freadman, M. (1988) Why animals have different muscle fibre types, *Nature*, **335**, 824–827.

Wardle, C. S., Videler, J. J. and Altringham, J. D. (1995) Tuning in to fish swimming waves: body form, swimming mode and muscle function, *Journal of Experimental Biology*, **198**, 1629–1636.

Webb, P. W. (1984) Form and function in fish swimming, *Scientific American*, **251**, 58–68.

Wellnhofer, P. (1991) *The Illustrated Encyclopedia of Pterosaurs*, Salamander, London.

ANSWERS TO QUESTIONS

Chapter 2

Question 2.1

(a)   False. In some fish, these fins do generate lift, but in others, they are used for manoeuvring, e.g. as in the John Dory, or for rowing, as in the stickleback.

(b)   False. Bending of the body results from the contraction of several myotomes on just one side of the body (see Figure 2.2).

(c)   False. Forward thrust in tunas is achieved mainly by strong movements of the caudal fin but this itself is moved by the muscles in the main trunk, and the force is transmitted via tendons.

(d)   True, although there are exceptions. Fins with a low AR have the advantage of being less prone to stalling.

(e)   True. This mode of swimming is intermediate between that of the eel and that of tunas. The salmon provides one example of this kind of swimming.

(f)   False. In order to accelerate, thrust generated by the fish must exceed the drag. The thrust that a fish generates is, at constant speed, equal to the drag forces resisting forward movement.

(g)   True. A fish is neutrally buoyant when the average density of the body tissues is equal to that of water.

(h)   True. The fins act like hydrofoils and, in order to provide lift, there must be a difference in the pressure above and below the fin. If the fish is stationary, no pressure difference is created and the fish sinks. During forward swimming, the fin is operated at an angle of incidence to the water, thereby creating a pressure difference, and hence lift.

(i)   True. Figure 2.10 shows that tiny vortices are set up by the projecting ctenoid scales and by the periodic movement of water to and from the sub-dermal spaces.

Question 2.2

$0.77\,\text{BL}\,\text{s}^{-1}$. The fish moves $16 \times 10^5\,\text{cm}$ in $8 \times 60 \times 60$ seconds. This is $55\,\text{cm}\,\text{s}^{-1}$, which should be divided by the stated body length, $72\,\text{cm}$.

Question 2.3

(a)   Burst swimming. Such a high speed could not be maintained indefinitely in a fish of this size. Note that $20\,\text{BL}\,\text{s}^{-1}$ by a 1 m long fish is $20\,\text{m}\,\text{s}^{-1}$, which is equivalent to $72\,\text{km}\,\text{h}^{-1}$.

(b)   Cruise swimming. This is close to the estimate given in the text for migrating longfin tuna.

(c)   Burst swimming. Such high speeds cannot be maintained for long periods but are typical of small fish for brief periods.

(d)   Cruise swimming. This is the maximum swimming speed that such a fish can attain without accumulating a significant requirement for recovery oxygen. Faster speeds are only maintained for limited periods.

Question 2.4

(a)   True. Swimming at speeds in excess of $4\,BL\,s^{-1}$ can be maintained for only a few minutes and the time taken for recovery oxygen uptake can be as long as 2–3 hours.

(b)   True. This is evident from Figures 2.21 and 2.22. Note that in fish, basal metabolic rate corresponds to oxygen consumption at zero speed, when the fish displays minimal activity.

(c)   True. Aerobic metabolic scope cannot simply be regarded as an index of an animal's ability to perform work, but it is a measure of the capability of the animal to increase the uptake and utilization of oxygen. Figure 2.22 shows how the aerobic metabolic scope of the salmon depends on temperature.

(d)   False. The precise factors that influence the duration of burst swimming are not fully known but the levels of stored glycogen are likely to be important, because this is the major substrate for anaerobic glycolysis.

(e)   False, at least this appears to be so on the evidence given in Figure 2.22. The figures quoted in Table 2.1 reveal that only air-breathing homeotherms show a completely different order of aerobic competence.

(f)   True. On the basis of evidence presented in Section 2.4.1, this seems a fair assumption. Note that many reptiles may increase their aerobic metabolic scope by operating at a somewhat higher temperature than fish. Most fish, unlike birds, are at an advantage because they live in a buoyant medium that permits immediate rest at any time for the uptake of recovery oxygen.

Chapter 3

Question 3.1

(a)   White. All red fibres are multiply innervated. White fibres can be multiply or focally innervated.

(b)   White. In this muscle a greater proportion of the fibre is composed of myofibrils and there are fewer mitochondria than in red muscle.

(c)   Red. The fibres are all multiply innervated. The breakdown of stored lipids releases fatty acids which can be oxidized to release energy—an aerobic process.

(d)   Red. Citrate synthetase is an enzyme responsible for an early step in the TCA cycle and cytochromes play a role in oxidative phosphorylation. Both these enzymes are therefore likely to be found in muscle with a high aerobic potential.

(e)   White. The trout is one example of a teleost where white muscle has a significant aerobic potential. In the light of (d) above, one would therefore expect trout white muscle to show aerobic metabolism at sustainable swimming speeds.

(f)   White. In this species, white muscle is probably used only at burst speeds.

Question 3.2

A is a sedentary bottom-dwelling angler fish; B is the mackerel; C is the unidentified active swimmer that uses enlarged pectoral fins.

You should have predicted that fast, constant swimmers that use their trunk musculature to power forward movement are likely to have relatively large amounts of red muscle, as is the case with mackerel. In fish that are not adapted to swim constantly, red muscle is likely to be less abundant, as in the angler fish. These measurements refer to the myotomes of the trunk musculature, and therefore where movement is achieved by fins rather than trunk musculature, one might expect that the red muscle content of the myotomes would be low.

Question 3.3

(a)   Glycogen has to be rapidly mobilized at the start of burst swimming and the muscle has a relatively poor capillary supply. Blood-borne factors may therefore be ineffective and a mechanism linked to the onset of nervous stimulation may be more appropriate.

(b)   You should recall from Chapter 2 that small fish move at relatively high speeds by virtue of their high tailbeat frequencies. (It has been calculated that the myotomes on either side of a 10 cm sprat are required to activate, contract and relax in only 30 ms.) In such cases, parvalbumins are likely to be particularly important in promoting rapid relaxation, which means that the muscle is able to contract and relax in very rapid cycles.

Question 3.4

(e) is accurate.

(a) is not true. It is no longer widely accepted that lactate is exported as a gluconeogenic substrate; much of the accumulated lactate is oxidized although it is possible that some is converted into glucose within white muscle.

(b) is not true because gluconeogenesis (the conversion of lactate to glucose) does require oxygen, albeit indirectly, because it utilizes ATP, which is depleted after exercise and which has to be restored by extra oxidative metabolism during recovery.

(c) is not true. PEP carboxykinase is absent or its activity is very slight in red muscle.

(d) is not true. Most lactic acid seems to be retained during burst swimming.

(f) is not true. The sparse circulation of white muscle, together with the tendency of white muscle to retain lactate, makes it unlikely that lactate is exported to red muscle.

Question 3.5

(a)   A range of fibres with different contraction speeds are required for fish to swim over a wide range of speeds. White fibres produce maximum power at tailbeat frequencies between 5 and 8 Hz. At these frequencies, the twitch kinetics and shortening velocities of red fibres are too slow to generate net positive work.

(b)   White fibres have a four-fold higher gearing ratio than red fibres. This means that white fibres need only shorten one quarter as much as red fibres for a given curvature of the body. The advantage of this is that the white muscle fibres can power movement while shortening at a rate of 5 lengths s^{-1} which is well below v_{max}. It also means that white fibres can generate maximum force at body curvatures that are characteristic of movements associated with burst activity by fish.

(c)   As a result of this, the timing of muscle activation in relation to fibre length varies systematically down the body. Muscle in the anterior myotomes is activated whilst the fibres are shortening and power output is positive throughout the tail beat cycle. However, fibres in myotomes towards the caudal fin are activated whilst lengthening and therefore initially produce negative work. Activating muscle fibres whilst they are lengthening dramatically increases their stiffness, thereby enabling the caudal myotomes at the posterior to transmit the power from the rostral myotomes to the tail blade.

Question 3.6

(a)   False. A wide variety of fish have heat exchangers, although tunas are the best studied. In particular, a number of sharks (i.e. elasmobranchs), including the notorious great white shark, have muscle or visceral retia.

(b)   True. Venous blood is cooled as it moves towards the posterior cardinal vein and this vessel conveys blood to the heart.

(c)   False. Those tunas, such as the skipjack, which possess heat exchangers have tissue temperatures that are above ambient, which means that they are not true poikilotherms. Moreover, they are endotherms because they produce and conserve significant amounts of metabolic heat, and may even be able to thermoregulate to some degree.

(d)   False. A proportion of the heat energy transformed by glycolysis could be released as heat, although the amounts would be smaller than that from fully aerobic tissue. However, in tuna, white muscle does have significant aerobic potential, and some tunas possess heat exchangers in the white muscle that would enable them to conserve such heat.

(e)   True. The mechanisms that conserve heat inevitably reduce the rate of heat loss to the exterior. A more stable body temperature may be an advantage in the wild.

(f)   False. Note that the diffusive flow of oxygen increases only fractionally as tissue temperatures increase. However, facilitated diffusion (oxygen bound to myoglobin) does increase significantly.

(g)   False. Being warm is not the only way to achieve high swimming speeds. For example, the wahoo can swim as fast as many tunas (as can the Pacific blue marlin), yet lacks heat exchangers and is a genuine poikilotherm. However, it may be that warm muscles are essential for sustained high-speed cruising with a substantial aerobic component.

It suggests that the central heat exchanger is extremely effective. If this were not so, the heat contained in the dorsal aorta would be transferred to the muscles via the segmental arteries that arise from the dorsal end of the rete. In this experiment heat was transferred from the arterial to the venous blood within the rete. This is the reverse of the usual heat flow but it shows how effective the process of heat transfer can be. Remember that blood flows from the posterior cardinal vein towards the heart and then along the ventral aorta, where blood can readily be sampled. The fact that most of the heat contained in the pulse appears in the ventral aorta also shows that most of the blood that passes along the dorsal aorta is directed through the rete, perhaps as much as 80% of the blood flow.

Only (f) and (g) provide limited evidence for thermoregulation.

(a)   This is evidence only that tunas can conserve metabolic heat. Thermoregulation implies the ability to vary the extent of heat conservation at different ambient temperatures.

(b)   Increasing metabolic rate is the conventional response of mammals to cold stress but, on current evidence, tunas do not display it.

(c)   This is a remarkable and unusual ability—in conventional poikilotherms the metabolic rate increases as the animal gets warmer. However, it tells us little about whether the skipjack maintains a stable body temperature as water temperature varies. It will certainly get round the problem of thermal runaway, and reduce the risks of acquiring an excessive heat load at high ambient temperatures. However, skipjack will still face the problem of heating up during bouts of intense activity.

(d)   Such an observation could be explained by the substantial thermal inertia of bluefin tuna. If bluefin produce a lot of metabolic heat, which is lost to the surrounding water very slowly, a stable core temperature may not necessarily indicate physiological thermoregulation.

(e)   This is shown in Figure 3.8. This information alone cannot be regarded as good evidence for thermoregulation and may result from large thermal inertia, as described in (d).

(f)   This represents thermoregulation by behavioural means rather than physiological methods, but the end result is the same. If this observation were to be confirmed, then it suggests that at high ambient temperatures the skipjack tuna's scope for activity would be very limited.

(g)   This provides limited support for the idea of physiological thermoregulation. In fact, in some skipjack tuna, excess temperatures fall when swimming speed is increased. The extent of heat production would be expected to increase in line with an increase in swimming speed so the absence of a similar rise in excess temperature implies that some mechanism intervenes to increase the extent of heat loss (or to decrease heat generation) or both.

So, the results of (f) and (g) suggest that skipjack tuna can regulate their temperature by both behavioural and physiological means.

Chapter 4

(a)   False. Because gas within a swimbladder obeys Boyle's law, the amount of lift imparted (which depends on the volume of the bladder) varies with depth.

(b)   True. Fish that are neutrally buoyant enjoy a significant advantage in energetic terms.

(c)   True. The cuttlefish, which does have a rigid buoyancy tank, is a cephalopod mollusc.

(d)   True. This is the principle of vertical instability.

(e)   False. Oxygen is not directly moved by active transport in the swimbladder. However, in a strict sense, it is true that energy-requiring processes are involved, e.g. in the gas gland the production of lactate is energy- (and glucose-) dependent.

(f)   False. The oval is found in the closed swimbladder where it regulates the extent of gas loss into the general circulation.

(g)   False. Many of the fish that demonstrate vertical migration do not remain neutrally buoyant throughout their journey—they generate dynamic lift if they become denser than seawater.

(h)   True. We have not explored this area to a great degree but, for example, some of the sensory roles of the swimbladder (e.g. sound reception) might depend on the maintenance of a constant volume.

(a)   At great depths, the gradient of gas partial pressure across the swimbladder wall is very high and the loss of gas by diffusion could be a major problem. The thick guanine layer substantially reduces loss of gas by diffusion.

(b)   Counter-current multiplication is probably more effective if the rete is long, with the result that the gradient of partial pressure along the rete becomes sufficiently great to move the gas into the swimbladder. A large rete is also a more effective 'lock' to prevent the loss of gas by diffusion.

(c)   The gas gland produces lactate, and the most obvious way of doing so is by glycolysis. Lactate dehydrogenase promotes the formation of lactate from pyruvate.

(d)   This high nitrogen content may in part be the result of preferential absorption of the more soluble carbon dioxide and oxygen from the mixture of gases that was initially secreted into the swimbladder. However, remember that salting-out of inert gases like nitrogen can occur and these may be concentrated by counter-current multiplication.

(e)   Carbon dioxide is a highly soluble gas, so, although the gas may be secreted into the swimbladder at a high rate, it usually disappears rapidly.

(f)   This is exactly what one would expect if lactic acid was produced by the gas gland and diffused into the outgoing blood. Lactate diffuses (or is transported) from the venous to the arterial vessels, so that lactate concentration in the venous vessels falls as blood moves from the gas gland, but levels in the arterial vessels increase as this blood approaches the gas gland.

(g) Freshwater fish need somewhat larger swimbladder volumes to attain neutral buoyancy (other things being equal) than do marine fish. For the same reason, extremely large amounts of stored lipid would be required to impart neutral buoyancy in freshwater fish, and the extra bulk may be prohibitive, perhaps because of increased drag.

Question 4.3

The correct statements in proper sequence are (c), (f) and (h) (these happen simultaneously), and (d).

(a) is untrue because the P_{O_2} is only about 20 kPa and at this stage most of the contained oxygen is bound to haemoglobin.

(b) is untrue because the oval in the closed swimbladder is a site of gas loss, not secretion.

(c) is true and accurately summarizes the condition of the blood as it enters the rete.

(d) is true and describes events that occur as the blood flows along the venous capillaries, when some lactic acid is diffusing into the arterial channels.

(e) is untrue. The acidification of the blood produces an immediate elevation of oxygen partial pressure, via the Root effect. Thus a significant increase in P_{O_2} comes from acidification alone; counter-current effects multiply this primary effect.

(f) is true because the diffusion of lactic acid into the arterial capillaries causes a Root effect, with a consequent unloading and elevation of P_{O_2} before blood reaches the gas gland.

(g) is untrue, because salting-out reduces the solubility of gases and raises their partial pressures.

(h) is true, because an elevated P_{O_2} in the venous capillaries results in diffusion of oxygen into the arterial capillaries, which is the first step in the generation of the multiplication effect.

(i) is false. The dissociation of oxyhaemoglobin ensures that the partial pressure of oxygen in the venous capillaries is relatively high, although there is almost complete equilibrium by the time the blood leaves the rete. However, the total oxygen content of venous blood is lower because of the unloading of oxyhaemoglobin.

Question 4.4

(a) Because of Boyle's law, considerable percentage changes in the volume of the swimbladder may occur with only modest changes in depth near the surface. The lift generated by the bladder would therefore change significantly as a fish moved up and down. This is not a problem for fish living right at the surface or those that do not change depth significantly.

(b) For fish that live at considerable depths, the percentage changes in swimbladder volume (and lift) that occur with depth change are relatively slight, but the problems of secreting and conserving gas are formidable. Other vertically migrating fish have abandoned gas as a source of static lift because of the considerable problems of regulating buoyancy over a substantial vertical range.

Chapter 5

Question 5.1

(a)   False. The aspect ratio of a wing describes its profile, not its cross-sectional area.

(b)   False. Increasing the angle of incidence increases lift, up to the point where the wing stalls.

(c)   True. Both induced and profile drag arise from the active movement of the wings. In gliding flight there will also be profile drag, but not induced drag.

Question 5.2

(a)   The wing has a high aspect ratio and a swept-back appearance. It comes from a sparrow, a bird that is built for high speed flight.

(b)   The wing has a low aspect ratio and the feathers are spread at the wing-tips. This wing is from an eagle, a bird that soars over land.

Question 5.3

The supracoracoideus muscle contracts and *elevates* the wing tip by rotating the head of the humerus in its joint with the coracoid bone. Contraction of the pectoral muscle *depresses* the wing by pulling the head of the humerus down towards the sternum. Depressing the wing exerts a force on the head of the humerus. At the bottom of the downstroke, the supracoracoideus muscle starts to contract again.

Question 5.4

The two techniques that you could have described are the use of sawdust particles suspended in the air and the use of helium bubbles. In both cases, the bird flies in the dark and is illuminated by photographic flash light. The photographs of the wake provide a visual representation of the forces exerted on the air by the bird, so photographs can be used to make measurements of flight parameters in a free-flying bird.

Question 5.5

The two gaits observed in birds are the continuous vortex gait and the vortex ring gait. Birds with long, thin wings, such as kestrels change from a vortex ring to a continuous vortex gait as their flight speed increases.

Question 6.1

The distinction between parachuting flight and gliding flight depends upon the angle of descent to the horizontal. If the angle is less than 45°, then the animal is described as gliding.

Question 6.2

Only (a), the flying snake, is a parachutist. The flying lizard, flying squirrel, flying fish and the hyalid frog are all gliders.

Large birds exploit thermals and use slope-soaring strategies, but these methods are not available to nocturnal or non-oceanic animals. There are no oceanic bats and very few are not nocturnal. You might also have mentioned that bats are insectivorous and frugivorous, which limits the range of habitats they can occupy. Also, since their hindlimbs are incorporated into their wings, bats roost upside down and this may limit their possible overall size.

You should have used the equation given in Section 6.5.3:

Cost of transport, $C = P/mgv$

Bird	Mass, m/kg	Flight speed, v/m s^{-1}	Power output, P/W	Cost of transport, C/W kg^{-1} m^{-1}
kestrel	0.20	8.1	1.8	0.113
lapwing	0.21	9.1	2.7	0.144
mallard	1.05	13.7	18.7	0.133

From the table, the lower the value for the cost of transport in the final column, the more efficient is the bird. Thus the kestrel is the most efficient. You might also have commented on the fact that the heavier mallard is more efficient than the lapwing, which is probably a consequence of its higher flight speed.

ACKNOWLEDGEMENTS

The Course Team would like to thank Professor Jeremy Rayner (University of Bristol), Professor McNeil Alexander (University of Leeds) and David Haley (British Aerospace) for their help and advice with this book.

Grateful acknowledgement is made to the following sources for permission to reproduce material in this book:

Figures

Figure 2.1: Nursall, J. R. (1956) The lateral musculature and the swimming of fish, *The Proceedings of the Zoological Society of London*, **126**(1), pp. 127–143, Zoological Society of London; *Figures 2.2, 2.10, 2.15, 2.17, 4.4, 4.6, 4.13*: Bone, Q. and Marshall, N. B. (1982) *Biology of Fishes*, Chapman and Hall; *Figures 2.3, 2.4, 2.5*: Lindsey, C. C. (1978) Form, function and locomotory habits in fish, in Hoar, W. S. and Randall, D. J. (eds) *Fish Physiology*, Volume VII, © 1978 Academic Press; *Figure 2.7*: Alexander, R. (1969) The innervation of muscle fibres in the myotomes of fishes, *Journal of the Marine Biological Association*, **49**, pp. 263–290, Cambridge University Press; *Figure 2.9*: Hertel, H. (1966) *Structure, Form and Function*, Van Nostrand Reinhold; *Figures 2.11(c), 3.6*: Videler, J. J. (1993) *Fish Swimming*, Chapman and Hall; *Figure 2.18*: Illustration by Prentiss, T. from Brett, J. R. (1964) The swimming energetics of salmon, *Scientific American*, August 1964, pp. 82–83. Copyright © 1964 by Scientific American, Inc. All rights reserved; *Figures 2.19, 2.20, 2.21, 2.22*: Reprinted from *Respiration Physiology*, **14**, Brett, J. R., The metabolic demand for oxygen in fish and other vertebrates, © 1972 with kind permission from Elsevier Science – NL, Sara Burgerhartstraat 25, 1055 KV Amsterdam, The Netherlands; *Figures 2.23, 2.24*: Block, B. A., Booth, D. and Carey, F. G. (1992) Direct measurement of swimming speeds and depth of blue marlin, *Journal of Experimental Biology*, **166**, pp. 267–284, Company of Biologists Ltd; *Figure 2.25*: Smith, G. W. (1981) Orientation and efficiency in the offshore movements of returning Atlantic salmon, *Scottish Fisheries Research Report No 21*, reproduced with the permission of The Scottish Office Agriculture, Environment and Fisheries Department Marine Laboratory; *Figures 2.26, 2.27*: Reprinted from *Journal of Fish Biology*, **39**, pp. 325–345, Lucas, M. C., Priede, I. G., Armstrong, J. D., Gindy, A. N. Z. and Vera, L. de, Direct measurements of metabolism, activity and feeding behaviour of pike, *Esox lucius* L. in the wild, by use of heart telemetry, copyright © 1991, by permission of the publisher Academic Press Limited London; *Figure 3.1*: Bone, Q. (1975) Muscular and energetic aspects of fish swimming, in Wu, T. Y., Brokaw, C. J. and Brennan, C. (eds) *Swimming and Flying in Nature*, Volume 2, by permission of Plenum Publishing Corporation and the author; *Figure 3.2(a)*: Courtesy of Professor I. A. Johnston; *Figure 3.2(b)*: Courtesy of Dr Q. Bone; *Figure 3.4*: Johnston, I. A. and Moon, T. W. (1980) Exercise training in skeletal muscle of brook trout (*Salvelinas fontinalis*), *Journal of Experimental Biology*, **87**, pp. 177–194, Company of Biologists Ltd; *Figure 3.5*: Rome, L. C. and Sosnicki, A. A. (1991) Myofilament overlap in swimming carp, II Sarcomere length changes during swimming, *American Journal of Physiology*, **260**, C289–296, American Physiological Society; *Figure 3.7*: Altringham, J. D., Wardle, C. and Smith, C. I.

(1993) Myotomal muscle function at different locations in the body of a swimming fish, *Journal of Experimental Biology*, **182**, pp. 191–206, Company of Biologists Ltd; *Figure 3.8*: Stevens, E. D. and Neil, W. H., Body temperature relations of tunas, especially skipjack, in Hoar, W. S. and Randall, D. J. (eds) *Fish Physiology,* Volume VII, © 1978, Academic Press, Inc.; *Figure 3.10*: Dewar, H., Graham, J. B. and Brill, J. W. (1994) Studies of tropical tuna swimming performance in a large water tunnel, II Thermoregulation, *Journal of Experimental Biology*, **192**, pp. 33–44, Company of Biologists Ltd; *Figure 3.11*: Carey, F. G., Teal, J. M., Kanwisher, J. W. and Lawson, K. O. (1971) Warm-bodied fish, *American Zoologist*, **11**(i), pp. 137–145, American Society of Zoologists; *Figure 3.12*: Stevens, E. D., Lam, H. M. and Kendall, J. (1974) Vascular anatomy of the counter-current heat exchanger of skipjack tuna, *Journal of Experimental Biology*, **61**, pp. 145–153, Company of Biologists Ltd; *Figure 3.13*: Carey, F. G. (1982) Warm fish, in Taylor, C. R., Johanson, K. and Bolis, L., *A Companion to Animal Physiology*, pp. 216–233, Cambridge University Press; *Figure 3.14*: Johnston, I. A. and Brill, R. (1984) Thermal dependence of contractile properties of single skinned muscle fibres from Antarctic and various warm water marine fishes including Skipjack Tuna (*Katsuwonus pelamis*) and Kawakawa (*Euthynnus affinis*), *Journal of Comparative Physiology*, B **155**, pp. 63–70, © Springer Verlag GmbH & Co. KG; *Figures 4.7, 4.12*: Blaxter, J. H. S. and Tytler, P., Physiology and function of the swim bladder, in Lowenstein, O. (ed.) *Advances in Comparative Physiology and Biochemistry*, Volume 7, p. 311–367, Academic Press, Inc.; *Figures 4.8, 4.9*: Denton, E. J. (1961) The buoyancy of fish and cephalopods, in Butler, J. A. V., Katz, B. and Kirkle, R. E. (eds) *Progress in Biophysics and Biophysical Chemistry*, Volume II, Pergamon Press; *Figure 4.10*: Denton, E. J. (1974) *Buoyancy in marine animals*, by permission of Oxford University Press; *Figure 4.11*: Root, R. W. (1931) The respiratory function of the blood of marine fishes, *Biological Bulletin*, **61**(3), p. 433, Marine Biological Laboratory; *Figure 5.4*: Rayner, J. M. V. (1981) Flight adaptations in vertebrates, *Symposium of the Zoological Society, London*, **48**, pp. 137–172, Zoological Society; *Figure 5.7*: Rayner, J. M. V. (1990) The mechanics of flight and bird migration performance, in Gwinner, E. *Bird Migration*, © Springer Verlag GmbH & Co. KG; *Figures 5.9, 5.10, 6.12*: Alexander, R. M. (1982) *Locomotion of Animals*, Chapman and Hall; *Figures 5.12, 5.13*: Freethy, R. (1982) *How Birds Work*, Blandford Press, by permission of Cassell; *Figures 5.17, 5.18:* Reprinted with permission from Jenkins Jr, F. A., Dial, K. P. and Goslow Jr, G. E. (1988) A cineradiographic analysis of bird flight: the wishbone in starlings is a spring, *Science*, **241**, pp. 1495–1498. Copyright 1988 American Association for the Advancement of Science; *Figure 5.19*: Courtesy of Dr Nikolai Kokshaysky; *Figures 5.21, 5.22, 6.13, 6.14*: Elder, H. Y. and Trueman, E. R. (1980) *Aspects of Animal Behaviour, Seminar Series, Society of Experimental Biology*, **5**, Cambridge University Press; *Figures 6.1, 6.9*: From Kenneth V. Kardong, *Vertebrates*, copyright © 1995 The McGraw-Hill Companies, Inc. Reprinted by permission. All rights reserved; *Figure 6.5*: From *Exploring Biomechanics* by Alexander, R. M. © 1992 by Scientific American Library. Used with permission of W. H. Freeman and Company; *Figures 6.7, 6.10*: Norberg, U. M. (1981) Flight, morphology and ecological niche in some birds and bats, *Symposium of the Zoological Society, London*, **48,** Zoological Society; *Figure 6.8*: Pennycuik, C. J. (1971) Gliding flight of the dog-faced bat *Rousettus aegyptiacus* observed in a wind tunnel, *Journal of Experimental Biology*, **55**, pp. 833–845, Company of Biologists Ltd.

Plates

Cover and Plate 5.1: Courtesy of Dr David Robinson; *Plates 6.1(a)*, *6.3*: Courtesy of Heather Angel Biofotos; *Plates 6.1(b)*, *6.1(d)*: Courtesy of Oxford Scientific Films/Michael Leach; *Plate 6.1(c)*: Courtesy of Ardea/Jean-Paul Ferrero; *Plate 6.1(e)*: Courtesy of Oxford Scientific Films/Isaac Kehimkab; *Plate 6.1(f)*: Courtesy of Oxford Scientific Films/Nick Bergkessel; *Plate 6.2*: Courtesy of Ardea; *Plate 6.4*: Courtesy of Heather Angel Biofotos/Ian Took; *Plate 6.5*: Courtesy of Oxford Scientific Films.

INDEX